Leisure and Recreation Studies
Series Editors: Stanley Parker and Sarah Gregory

2 Leisure and Work

Leisure and Recreation Studies

Leisure and Work

Stanley Parker

London
George Allen & Unwin
Boston   Sydney

George Allen & Unwin (Publishers) Ltd
40 Museum Street, London WC1A 1LU, UK

George Allen & Unwin (Publishers) Ltd,
Park Lane, Hemel Hempstead, Herts HP2 4TE, UK

Allen & Unwin, Inc.,
9 Winchester Terrace, Winchester, Mass. 01890, USA

George Allen & Unwin Australia Pty Ltd,
8 Napier Street, North Sydney, NSW 2060, Australia

First published in 1983

This book is an extensive revision of an earlier work,
The Future of Work and Leisure, published by Granada Publishing.

British Library Cataloguing in Publication Data

Parker, Stanley
    Leisure and work. – (Leisure and recreation studies; 2)
1. Leisure
I. Title   II. Series
306'.48   GV174
ISBN 0-04-301162-4
ISBN 0-04-301163-2 Pbk

Library of Congress Cataloging in Publication Data

Parker, Stanley Robert.
    Leisure and work.
(Leisure and recreation studies; 2)
Rev. ed. of: The future of work and leisure. 1971.
Bibliography: p.
Includes index.
1. Work. 2. Leisure   I. Title.   II. Series.
HD4904.6.P37   1983   306'.36   83-11820
ISBN 0-04-301162-4
ISBN 0-04-301163-2 (pbk.)

Set in 10 on 11 point Bembo by Computape (Pickering) Ltd
and printed in Great Britain
by Billing and Sons Ltd, London and Worcester

Contents

111287

Preface

It is twelve years since I wrote *The Future of Work and Leisure* and for several years it has been out of print. During that time much has been said and written on the subject of work and leisure: more research has been carried out, earlier ideas have been re-evaluated and fresh hypotheses put forward. Industrial societies have, at least in some senses, continued to move away from work and – more questionably – towards leisure. Unemployment has grown, time at work has been reduced for many (but not all) employees, and public and private provision for leisure has increased. In academic and information terms, courses of leisure and recreation studies have been set up, a multi-disciplinary Leisure Studies Association has been formed in Britain, and new publications in book and journal form have increased from a trickle to a moderate stream.

The need for reasonably comprehensive and up-to-date treatment, in a series of books on leisure and recreation studies, of leisure in relation to work gives me the opportunity to revise and expand upon what I wrote in *The Future of Work and Leisure*. This revision and expansion is intentionally selective. My treatment of some topics, such as work and leisure in history and non-industrial societies, remains basically unchanged. But with other topics, notably the social effects of micro-technology and the work–leisure relationship for different groups in contemporary society, developments have taken place which demand a more extended discussion than previously.

In the earlier book I put forward some tentative views, based upon my own research and that of others, on the relationship between work and leisure, both as it is in our society and as it could be if certain policies were adopted and changes made. Nothing I said was fundamentally new, although I aimed to make a contribution to our state of knowledge and to the debate on what we should do about the situation facing us. The publication of that book provoked some critical reaction and some research, the consequences of which oblige me to reformulate in the present book some of what I had written. This is an entirely healthy and progressive process. When writing of the role of leisure and work in our own lives and in the structure of the society in which we live, we are dealing only partly with facts and figures: more important, we are entering into a debate about *values*, about different ways of interpreting the knowledge we acquire and using it to achieve the individual and societal goals we believe to be desirable.

Introduction

We hear quite a lot these days about the promise (or threat) of more leisure. We hear less about the problem of work – except in the context of growing unemployment. Yet both leisure and work are really part of the same problem, and a careful consideration of all the issues involved shows that we are unlikely to go far in solving the one without tackling the other. The *quantity* of leisure time is increasing for many people – although not at such a dramatic rate as some observers would have us believe – because working time is getting less. Shorter working weeks, longer holidays, a longer period of retirement because we tend to give up employment earlier and live longer – all these things are giving us more leisure. Not everyone, however, is participating in this leisure boom. People in some occupations are finding that work is as demanding as ever. The people who find work most absorbing are those who have least leisure, whereas those in more or less routine jobs (who, according to some commentators, have the least resources for using leisure time creatively) are finding more time on their hands.

Of course the experiences of work and leisure by individual men and women have to be looked at against the social and economic background of the larger community of which they are part. Faced with the choice of more leisure time or more income, a good many British workers still choose more income from overtime, a second job, or do-it-yourself activities which are hardly leisure. This is mainly because the income from a basic working week at many jobs is still too low to afford a decent standard of living. The time may well come, however, when the development of microelectronics and other technological advances will mean that the individual's choice between more work or more leisure need no longer be dictated by economic necessity. We may grumble about certain aspects of our jobs, but it is only when we are made redundant or forced to retire that many of us realise how big a part the job played in our lives. Those of us who are lucky enough to be employed doing the kind of work that we should choose to do even if we were financially free do not need to make such a big adjustment – the end of employment does not mean the end of *work* of a kind we thought worthwhile. But others among us who are denied the opportunity of working in this way may well find that too much leisure is an even bigger problem than too much work.

Some people look on leisure and work in the same way as the

hedonist philosophy looks on pleasure and pain – the one to be sought after eagerly and the other to be avoided like the plague. But research in the various social sciences shows that both work *and* leisure are necessary to a healthy life and a healthy society, though whether these two spheres need to be as separate as they are for most individuals today is debatable. The idea that work cannot be made a source of interest and even fulfilment for the mass of people and that we should therefore pin our hopes on leisure is just as one-sided as the view that work is the real business of life and that leisure is at best a servant of better work. Maximum human development in both work and leisure spheres requires that they be complementary and integrated, rather than that one be regarded as 'good' and the other as 'bad'.

When we *do* think of work as something unpleasant and to be avoided, this is usually because of the purpose for which it is done or the conditions under which it is done. If the purpose of work is simply to earn money in order to live, then both the employee and his employer tend to ignore the possibility of making work itself a more meaningful experience. Even trade unions, who claim to look after the interests of workers, largely ignore the possibility of making the experience of work more worthwhile in itself, while struggling to make it more remunerative and less time-consuming. This is typical of a society in which we have become used to the idea of exploiting human resources along with other resources. We may say that things are different when it comes to leisure. But life is of a piece, and men and women who are accustomed to being exploited in their work may find it hard to avoid being exploited in their leisure.

So we arrive at the proposition that the problem of leisure is also the problem of work. This does not mean that there is nothing we can do to improve leisure opportunities quite apart from anything we may do about the organisation of work. The need for better facilities for and information about different types of leisure activity is widely recognised, and as we hopefully move from a recessive to an expanding economy we shall be able to afford to spend a larger proportion of our incomes on leisure goods and services. But that would be to tackle only the material side of things. There is evidence that the people who are least involved in their work are also the least involved in their leisure – that frustration in one sphere goes along with frustration in another. To expect a change in one part of life which would not affect other parts is to assume a split that is not easy to make or to sustain, even if it is thought desirable.

It is tempting to believe that whatever differences there are between what men and women put into and get out of work and leisure are the result of their personalities or 'the sort of people they are'. Because those who think like this discount the effects of environment, they advocate that we should try to match 'types of person' to 'types of situation'. They overlook the possibility that, at least to some extent, people are shaped, changed, developed, or retarded by the types of situation into which they are put. But if we put men and women into categories at the beginning of their adult lives – if we say that some need work into which they can put a lot of themselves, while others need only a satisfying leisure life – then we are restricting their range of opportunities for a full and balanced life.

A programme designed to realise human potentialities would have both a work and a leisure aspect. In the work sphere employees (individually or through their unions or other associations) can demand more interesting work and a greater say in how it is organised. The apathy of many workers and the reluctance of management to let workers have a say in how things are run are obstacles to be overcome, but experiments in a few progressive enterprises show what can be done on a wider scale. A revaluation of leisure would need to complement such a revaluation of work. To most people, leisure means time during which they feel free to do whatever they want. Consequently it is thought to be wrong for a society to attempt to plan the leisure of its members. Up to a point we can, of course, choose to do what we like in our free time, but somehow we manage to spend much of our time and money as customers of one or other branch of the leisure industries, which are organised on the same lines as most factories and offices. If we are not encouraged to think for ourselves at school and at work, we are not likely to have the mental resources to think for ourselves in leisure time.

This book is a study of the relationship between people at work and people at play. It has both theoretical and practical aims: to contribute to the development of social science theory, including evaluating alternative views of man, society and social change; and to contribute to the solution of problems of leisure and work, by attempting to predict the likely outcome of alternative social policies.

In order to understand our present social situation and its possible future development, we need to know something of the past and of cultures besides our own. Accordingly I adopt, in the chapters that follow, a primarily sociological perspective, while recognising that the subject of leisure and work lends itself to approaches other than sociological ones. Psychology enters into it because the way in which people relate their leisure to their work or seek to separate these two spheres is to some extent a matter for individual choice. History and anthropology have something to contribute because meanings of work and leisure have changed through the ages and are even today different in various cultures. Philosophy and religion have a stake in this area because the quality and values of 'the good life' certainly involve some conception of how leisure and work make their separate or joint contributions to it. Social planning, too, is concerned – indeed, those of us who claim to be applied rather than merely theoretical sociologists may see the aim of all our knowledge as a contribution to the solution of social problems.

Sociology is concerned with relationships, and there are two types of relationship to be studied: the relationship between society's need for work to be done and for the benefits that its members may collectively derive from leisure; and the relationship between the functions of work and leisure to individuals themselves. The prevailing values attached to leisure must bear some relationship to the values attached to work, since, for most people in present society, leisure is only possible after work has first been done. Apart from any theoretical interest in the social and individual relationships involved in work and leisure, there is also a more practical concern about 'the problem of leisure', which, as I hope to show, in the long run also involves the problem of work. Some knowledge about the actual relationship between work and leisure in past and present societies should help us to predict what forms this relationship might take, given certain changes in the structure of society and/or in the prevailing set of values.

It is important to recognise the nature of the problems facing policy-makers in this field. Like all planners, they are concerned with establishing priorities and reconciling divergent interests. They *should* be trying to steer a course between *laissez-faire* and authoritarianism, between letting things take their own way (often a way determined by vested interests) and seeking to control people's lives from the cradle to the grave. The experience of working life is not usually thought of as a social problem. There is plenty of justified concern about helping people to get a job, training them for it, making conditions in it hygienic and safe for them, and compensating them if they lose it. But seldom is anything said about whether it is a job fit for human beings to do, whether it develops them as persons, whether it gives them anything beyond the pay packet and a feeling that time at work is time wasted. There is more interest in 'the problem of leisure', but too often this is defined narrowly as a problem only for certain minority groups such as teenagers or retired persons. The rest of us may not realise that we have a problem until we are shown a solution – that is, the steps that are required to change society so that more people are afforded more opportunities for a creative and satisfying work and leisure life.

It is only partly true to say that the subject of work and leisure has been neglected in discussions about the sort of society we are trying to build. The theme of work *as production* is often in the news. It is said that British people do not work hard enough compared with people in other countries or with the 'good old days' in this country; that management, by and large, does not know how to organise production efficiently; that it is still possible (or impossible) for people to 'get to the top' from humble beginnings by hard work, and so on. But the ways in which leisure engages the public attention are on a different plane altogether. It is said that what we need are more leisure facilities, more ways of filling our free time, that our children should be educated for leisure as well as (or even rather than) for work, and our older people educated in how to cope with retirement after a lifetime of employment.

Only rarely, however, are the problems of work and leisure looked at together. Sometimes an individual pauses in his daily round of activity to assess the balance of his life, to take stock and plan for the future. In the following pages I shall be looking at our *society* in this way; not at the whole of it (that would take many more pages) but at every aspect of the relationship between work and leisure. I shall draw on the researches and thoughts of many people who have had something to say on these matters.

At the outset it may help the reader to see the relevance of these studies to his own concern with work and leisure if they are briefly reviewed. First, there are the attempts to sort out what is meant by work and leisure in the pattern of life – no easy task, because there is much loose thinking and confusion in this field. Secondly, research into how people in societies other than our own relate the work and leisure parts of their lives – or whether, indeed, they make such a distinction at all – helps to put our own behaviour and ideas into perspective. Thirdly, there are different kinds of work and different kinds of leisure in our modern industrial society and we can learn a lot from surveys and other inquiries into how people in various circumstances tend to behave in and think about leisure and work. Fourthly, we have the theorists and philosophers who link definitions and concepts to people and situations and produce ideas about what work and leisure ought to be and to mean. Finally, the social planners try to find out what the needs of men and women for work and leisure are and put forward programmes to meet these needs.

All of these types of study contribute in one way or another to the form that society takes, and by knowing about them and taking part in the ongoing discussion of what they imply in our own lives each of us can help to shape our collective future.

1

Changing Definitions and Concepts

One of the difficulties of the English language is that words like 'leisure' and 'work' have such a wide variety of meanings. The *Oxford Dictionary* takes four columns to list the various usages of 'work' and gives a shorter, but still by no means clear, explanation of what 'leisure' is. It is tempting to argue that since the present words are used to mean so many different things it would be better to abandon them and to start from scratch with new terms which could be clearly defined. But we should still at some points have to translate these new terms back into their old equivalents, and probably this would, on balance, lead to even greater confusion. Our first task, then, is to sort out the various meanings of work and leisure and to see how they relate to each other.

Definitions of Work

To the individual in a modern industrial society such as ours, work is usually identified with the means of earning a living. In simpler societies the relationship between work and such basic necessities as food, clothing and shelter is a direct one for the individual or for a comparatively small group; they consume only what they are able to produce. The evolution of society through various forms of social production and ownership of property progressively breaks down the direct link between individual productive effort and consumption of goods and services. Hard physical labour is less and less required as machines take over more of the tasks of production and distribution. Fewer people are needed to produce the basic necessities of life, and the goods and services of the 'leisure industries' account for an increasing proportion of total production and employment.

It will be noticed that we have already used, besides work itself, four of its synonyms: production, effort, labour and employment. Sometimes the adjective 'productive' precedes 'work', but a too literal interpretation of 'productive' is misleading, since the *effort* to produce something is work irrespective of whether a 'product' results, and the rendering of services, no less than the production of goods, requires work. The distinction between the terms 'work', 'labour' and 'employment' is even more important. Only the last of these terms implies a social relationship, although it is sometimes used in the same non-social sense as work, for example, when we say that someone is 'self-employed'. The most common form of employment consists of an employer (individual or corporate body) hiring the working abilities of an employee during set hours. For the employee, this is the equivalent of *working time*, and it is relatively easy for him to distinguish this from *non-working time*, a part or the whole of which may be defined as leisure.

The other two concepts of work and labour have to do with *activity* rather than time. Both are often equated with employment, but while it is true that all employment implies work of some kind, the reverse is not necessarily so. Employment is work in the narrow sense of income-producing activity, but work has a wider biological and physiological meaning of purposeful and sustained action. Whereas employment may be contrasted with idleness or with work that is economically unremunerative or disinterested, work in its broad meaning is the opposite of rest.

Although 'labour' is often used as a synonym for work, Hannah Arendt (1958) has suggested that there is good reason for keeping the two concepts separate. She uses 'labour' to denote necessary activity assuring the survival of the individual and the species, and 'work' to denote an unnatural activity providing an 'artificial' world of things. She maintains that the necessity of 'making a living' (that is, employment) has reduced nearly all human activities to the level of labour:

> Whatever we do, we are supposed to do for the sake of 'making a living'; such is the verdict of society, and the number of people, especially in the professions, who might challenge it has decreased rapidly. The only exception society is willing to grant is the artist who, strictly speaking, is the only 'worker' left in a labouring society. The same trend to level down all serious activities to the status of making a living is manifest in present-day labour theories, which almost unanimously define labour as the opposite of play. As a result, all serious activities, irrespective of their fruits, are called labour, and every activity which is not necessary either for the life of the individual or for the life process of society is subsumed under playfulness. (p. 127)

Arendt equates labour with earning a living (employment) and contrasts both with work. Perhaps she is mistaken in supposing that all people today except artists are labourers rather than workers. But the distinction she draws is an important one and finds an echo in the remarks of one ex-miner:

> As I see it there are basically only two kinds of work. One is the sort that in the main is done for its own sake. Attached to it are no notions of bosses or clocks or profits or wages and usually it proves rewarding in itself. The other sort is that which is normally done in return for a weekly wage at docks, in factories, on building sites, down pits where one is a slave to timekeeping, norms, incentives, procedures. (Keenan, 1968, p. 276)

Definitions of Leisure

One of the chief problems of defining leisure is that it is very difficult to take an objective approach to the subject. Perhaps even more than in the case of work, the way in which someone defines leisure tends to be determined by his view of what it ought to be. There is an element of this even in the kind of definition which sees leisure as that part of time left over after work and perhaps also after other obligations have been met, because the judgement about where work leaves off and leisure begins is usually a subjective one. Between this kind of definition which concentrates on the dimension of *time*, and the openly normative definition which is concerned with quality of *activity* or being, there is an approach which seeks to combine the two. We may, therefore, conveniently review various definitions of leisure which fall into these three broad groups.

What may be called the 'residual' type of definition is concerned with what is to be taken out of total time in order that leisure alone should remain. Clearly the minimum that can be taken out of all time to leave only leisure is working time in the narrow sense of employment. Hunter (1961), author of a report on the findings of a study group on leisure, exemplifies this approach:

> 'Leisure' was not defined in this study, save tacitly to mean the hours when a man is not working primarily for money. Those hours have to include many things; household duties, rest, relaxation, social contact, family life, voluntary work, sport and hobbies and an opportunity for a man's mind and mood and whole being to move in a different world from the world of work and production. (p. 16)

George Soule (1957) makes a similarly broad distinction between sold and unsold time: 'What one does in sold time is "the job" ... Time not sold, "one's own time", "free time", is thought of as leisure, no matter what one does with it.'

Other residual definitions of leisure add items of varying degrees of precision to the basic employment exclusion to arrive at leisure time. Thus Edward Gross (1961) suggests that 'leisure refers to free time, free, that is, from the need to be concerned about maintenance'. George Lundberg (1934) defined leisure as 'the time we are free from the more obvious and formal duties which a paid job or other obligatory occupation imposes upon us', and, as if to apologise for the lack of objectivity in this definition, he added the thought that 'nearly all people can and do classify nearly all their activities according to these two categories [work and leisure] in a way that is deeply meaningful to themselves'. Giddens (1964) is more precise about what leisure excludes, defining it 'in a residual fashion, to denote that sphere of life not occupied in working, travelling to work or sleeping', while White (1955) excludes sleeping, eating and working from the realm of leisure.

The second group of definitions consists of those which start with a residual approach such as those above, but go on to include a positive description of its content or function, sometimes adding a prescriptive element. To Charles Brightbill (1963)

> leisure is time beyond that which is required for *existence*, the things which we must do, biologically, to stay alive (that is, eat, sleep, eliminate, medicate, and so on); and *subsistence*, the things we must do to make a living as in work, or prepare to make a living as in school, or pay for what we want done if we do not do it ourselves. Leisure is time in which our feelings of compulsion should be minimal. It is *discretionary* time, the time to be used according to our own judgment or choice. (p. 4)

This is a bold attempt to satisfy criteria both of content and of quality, but it fails on at least two counts: eating and sleeping sometimes contain discretionary, as opposed to biologically necessary, elements; and subsistence tasks and the use of time according to our own judgement or choice are not necessarily mutually exclusive. Incidentally, it may be questioned whether going to school is really to 'prepare to make a living' rather than to prepare to make a *life* (work and leisure).

Gist and Fava (1964) note the limitations of their own definition of leisure. According to them it is

> the time which an individual has free from work or other duties and which may be utilized for the purposes of relaxation, diversion, social achievement, or personal development. Like many other definitions, this one does not clearly demarcate leisure from non-

leisure, or leisure activity from activity that is obligatory; indeed, what is often considered leisure-time behaviour may be, in part, a response to social pressures or powerful inner drives, and may not therefore be a preferred form of behaviour. (p. 411)

A similar approach was taken by the seminar members of the International Group of the Social Sciences of Leisure, who drew up the following definition:

> Leisure consists of a number of occupations in which the individual may indulge of his own free will – either to rest, to amuse himself, to add to his knowledge or improve his skills disinterestedly or to increase his voluntary participation in the life of the community after discharging his professional, family and social duties. (Dumazedier, 1960, p. 527)

The chief advantage of these two definitions over that of Brightbill is that they do not try to combine two types of criteria to distinguish leisure from non-leisure in one step, but insist that what is leisure must pass two separate tests: it must be time free from obligations (though Gist and Fava appear to raise the philosophical question of whether activities are ever really freely chosen) and it must serve specific purposes such as relaxation or community participation.

One complex definition of leisure includes not only differentiation from economic activity but also a number of other criteria. Max Kaplan (1975) believes that leisure

> consists of relatively self-determined activity-experience that falls into one's economically free-time roles, that is seen as leisure by participants, that is psychologically pleasant in anticipation and recollection, that potentially covers the whole range of commitment and intensity, that contains characteristic norms and constraints, and that provides opportunities for recreation, personal growth and service to others. (p. 26)

But Kenneth Roberts (1978) prefers simplicity and argues that, although Kaplan's definition may convey certain qualities of leisure experience, it is unnecessarily elaborate and therefore confusing. No researcher has ever found it practical to work from so elaborate a definition. Also, whether leisure is psychologically pleasant and whether it results in personal growth and service to others are, according to Roberts, better regarded as hypotheses requiring investigation than issues to be resolved by definition.

The third group of definitions consists of those which are wholly prescriptive and normative. They stress the *quality* of leisure, though they may do this by contrasting it with the attributes of work. Although antecedents of normative leisure can be traced to even earlier civilisations, it was in ancient Greece that the concept evolved and was elaborated into a philosophy and a way of life for the privileged slave-owning section of the community. This traditional or classical view of leisure emphasises contemplation, enjoyment of self in search of knowledge, debate, politics and cultural enlightenment (Murphy, 1974).

Later, religious writers approached the question of leisure from a similarly normative standpoint. The Protestant view of leisure identifies it with qualities of refinement, holding it to be unique because it is often associated with spiritual or artistic values (Vontobel, 1945). A Catholic view as expressed by Josef Pieper (1952) is that leisure 'is a mental and spiritual attitude – it is not simply the result of external factors, it is not the inevitable result of spare time, a holiday, a weekend or a vacation. It is . . . an attitude of mind, a condition of the soul, and as such utterly contrary to the ideal of "work".' The disadvantage of this kind of definition is that it offers no objective criteria for making comparisons. If leisure is to be identified as an attitude of mind or a condition of soul we must ask: which attitude of mind and which condition of soul? Unless these states of mind and soul can be expressed in terms of certain attitudes or result in certain kinds of observable behaviour, they are unlikely to get us far in the search for what distinguishes leisure from non-leisure.

Not all normative definitions have a religious origin. Burch (1971), an American philosopher and social scientist, views leisure as that aspect of life which, in contrast with labour or work, permits one to have a relatively greater range of activity options. This does not mean that leisure is free of normative constraints, but rather that less formal, less bureaucratic constraints operate. Leisure as 'choosing time' suggests that discretion is the better part of one's constraints. Also, it is a definition general enough to include play, recreation and diversion as well as artistic production. In the same vein, Ross (1971) suggests that the more an individual can pursue an activity with few restrictions on his choice, time and spatial movement, the more we would consider him to be enjoying leisure.

When considering work, we found it necessary to distinguish it from associated concepts of labour and employment. It is equally necessary to distinguish leisure from allied concepts, particularly from that of free time. Although some writers take free time to mean the same as leisure, others insist that there is a qualitative difference. Thus, according to Sebastian DeGrazia (1962) free time is not the same as leisure:

Work is the antonym of free time. But not of leisure. Leisure and free time live in two different worlds. We have got in the habit of thinking them the same. Anybody can have free time. Free time is a realizable idea of democracy. Leisure is not fully realizable, and hence an ideal, not alone an idea. Free time refers to a special way of calculating a special kind of time. Leisure refers to a state of being, a condition of man, which few desire and fewer achieve. (pp. 7–8)

These conceptions of 'free time' as merely time and 'leisure' as an ideal state of being may be contrasted with the views of Herbert Marcuse, who virtually reverses the definitions of DeGrazia. According to Marcuse (1964):

the Welfare State is a state of unfreedom because its total administration is systematic restriction of (a) 'technically' available free time ... (*Footnote*: 'Free time', not 'leisure time'. The latter thrives in advanced industrial society, but it is unfree to the extent to which it is administered by business and politics.) (p. 49)

Both writers appear to be talking about true or 'free' leisure, but whereas DeGrazia defines it as leisure and calls into question the 'freedom' of free time, Marcuse defines it as free time and calls into question the freedom of leisure!

However, leaving this largely semantic problem aside, there is a further difficulty presented by the views of DeGrazia. To say that leisure and free time live in two different worlds is another way of saying that they are not measurable by the same criteria. It is a plea against treating them as interchangeable concepts. But the distinction is not confined to the area of non-work. It applies also in the work sphere. Some working time is 'paid' time, but you do not have to be an employee in order to do work and in that sense 'anyone can have working time'. Yet work as a certain kind of activity, a productive relationship between a person and his environment may, like leisure, be something which few in our present society desire and fewer achieve. The two worlds of time and activity are thus not the sole domains of work and leisure respectively, but are both dimensions of work *and* leisure.

Components of Life Space

'Life Space' means the total of activities or ways of spending time that people have. In considering the various definitions of work and leisure we have already seen that to allocate all the parts of life space either to work or to leisure would be a gross oversimplification. As Roberts

(1978) remarks, leisure shades imperceptibly into other spheres of life, making it impossible to measure exactly how much of it individuals have. Indeed, there is a strong case for conceiving of leisure as a continuous rather than as a discrete phenomenon. There may be some leisure in virtually any activity undertaken, even if it is not capable of being accurately identified and measured (Ennis, 1968; Gunter and Gunter, 1980).

Assuming, however, that it does make some sense to use the exhaustive categories of 'work' and 'non-work', this still does not enable us to say where the line between the two is to be drawn or what exceptions to the demarcation may need to be made for some purposes. Also, important differences exist within as well as between these two categories. A number of writers have suggested schemes for analysing the twenty-four hours in the average person's day into various categories. Instead of examining these schemes in detail, we may put the various categories that have been suggested into five main groups. This should make analysis easier, and it assumes that any differences among the categories in each group are fairly minor.

(1) *Work, working time, sold time, subsistence time.* Although, as we have already seen, 'work' has a wider meaning than employment, for the purpose of analysing life space it is usually identified with earning a living. If an employee is on piece rates then it is 'work', or more precisely the product of work, that he sells; if he is on time rates then he sells so much working time. However, these are both ways of measuring work *and* working time, and differ only in the way the remuneration is calculated. 'Subsistence time' lays emphasis on the purpose of work to the employee, that is, enabling him and his dependants to subsist.

(2) *Work-related time, work obligations.* Apart from actual working time, most people have to spend a certain amount of time travelling to and from the place of work and in preparing or 'grooming' themselves for work. In some cases, however, at least part of the travelling time may be regarded more as a form of leisure than as work-related – for example, time spent reading newspapers or books, chatting to fellow-travellers, or playing cards with them. Voluntary overtime and having a second job may also be regarded as related to the main working time rather than as part of it, as may activities in the no-man's land between work and leisure such as reading on the subject of one's work when at home, attending conferences or trade union meetings which have a social as well as a work side, and so on.

(3) *Existence time, meeting physiological needs.* This is the first of three non-work groups. We all have to spend a certain minimum of time on sleep and on the mechanics of living – eating, washing, eliminating, and so on. Beyond the minimum necessary for reasonably healthy

living, extra time spent on these things may be more like a leisure activity. Eating for pleasure, taking extra care with one's appearance for a party or social occasion, sexual activity beyond the call of purely physiological need, are some examples which show that the line between the satisfaction of 'existence' needs and leisure activities is not always easy to draw.

(4) *Non-work obligations, semi-leisure.* Joffre Dumazedier (1967) has coined the term *semi-leisure* to describe 'activities which, from the point of view of the individual, arise in the first place from leisure, but which represent in differing degrees the character of obligations'. The obligations are usually to other people, but may be to non-human objects such as pets or homes or gardens. Again, the line between obligation and leisure is not always clear and depends to a large extent on one's attitude to the activity. Gardening and odd-job work around the home can be a chore or an absorbing hobby, and playing with the children can be a duty or a delight.

(5) *Leisure, free time, spare time, uncommitted time, discretionary time, choosing time.* All the terms after 'leisure' describe some aspect of what is meant by leisure. We saw earlier that residual definitions of leisure give it as time free from various commitments and obligations, and that 'free' time is best regarded as a dimension of leisure. 'Spare' time is a slightly different idea, implying that, like a spare tyre, it is not normally in use but could be put to use. 'Uncommitted' time suggests a lack of obligations, of either a work or non-work character. 'Discretionary' or 'choosing' time is perhaps the essence of leisure, because it means time that we can use at our own discretion and according to our own choice.

From a careful study of the various schemes for analysing life space three points emerge:

(1) Time and activity are dimensions which are both present in all categories of life space, even where, for the sake of brevity, both are not always referred to.
(2) Between compulsory activities (in order to live or to earn a living) and freely chosen ones, some activities have the character of obligations. This applies to both work and non-work activities.
(3) Leisure implies relative freedom of choice, and it is possible to work during one's 'leisure' time.

Bearing these points in mind, a *time* scheme for the analysis of life space may be proposed (Figure 1.1). In this scheme work may be defined as the activity involved in earning a living, plus necessary subsidiary activities such as travelling to work. Work obligations include voluntary overtime, doing things outside normal working hours associated with the job or type of work that are not strictly necessary to a minimum acceptable level of performance in the job, or having a second job. The satisfaction of physiological needs follows the conventional definition of these needs. Non-work obligations are roughly what Dumazedier calls semi-leisure. Leisure is time free from obligations either to self or to others – time in which to do as one chooses.

Work time		Non-work time		
Work (employment)	Work obligations	Physiological needs	Non-work obligations	Leisure

Figure 1.1   *Time scheme for the analysis of life space.*

Time and activity are dimensions, or ways of measuring a variable. In analysing life space the crucial time variable seems to be whether a given space of time is work or not, while the main activity variable seems to be the extent to which the activity is constrained or freely chosen. The constraint may arise from within the individual himself or may be imposed on him by the way in which he lives. The elements in the above time scheme may be reordered and slightly modified into a two-dimensional time and activity scheme (Figure 1.2). Except for leisure, particular types of activity may be fairly clearly allocated to work or non-work time. Economic necessity constrains most men and many women under pension age to have one job (work), but only if they choose to value a higher standard of living above more free time need they do overtime or take a second job (work obligation). Similarly, in the non-work sphere the satisfaction of physiological needs is, in its own way, as necessary as work, but non-work obligations are only obligations within a prior context of freedom to choose; for example, a man can avoid non-work obligations connected with the conjugal family by staying single.

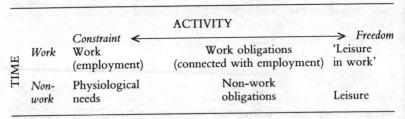

Figure 1.2   *Two-dimensional time and activity scheme.*

The position of leisure is rather special. It is clearly at the 'freedom' end of the constraint–freedom scale, but it need not be restricted to non-working time. We draw attention to this paradox when we say that someone else's way of choosing to spend leisure time looks to us more like hard work. 'Work' and 'leisure in work' may consist of the same activity; the difference is that the latter is chosen for its own sake. Thus mountaineering is work for the guide but leisure in work for the amateur climber. Leisure time and employment time cannot overlap, but there is no reason why some of the time that is sold as work should not be utilised by the seller (that is, the employee) for leisure-type activities, provided that the buyer (the employer or his agent) has no objection, or is ignorant of or cannot control the situation. In addition to such oases of leisure in the desert of the working day, there remains the point that leisure means *choice*, and so time chosen to be spent as work activity – though not involving the constraint of employment – can be leisure just as much as more conventional leisure activities.

Time is limited to the twenty-four hours in the day, but some human activities are such that two or more can take place at the same time. For example, the satisfaction of a physiological need, such as eating, can be accompanied by a leisure activity, such as listening to the radio. A chart of life space with only the time dimension has difficulty in coping with such simultaneous activities which fall into different categories. To overcome this difficulty the time budget people (Szalai, 1972) have used the concepts of primary and secondary activities and have added the duration of the total of secondary activities to the twenty-four hours in the day to give a total daily time budget of up to thirty-two hours for some groups. As well as allocating primary and secondary activities to the same space of time, we may allocate primary and secondary functions to the same activity. Thus activities which are primarily at the constraint end of the scale, such as employment, may involve in a secondary way the leisure-like element of freely chosen activity, in this case, the type of work we should like to do even if we had no need of employment.

One important qualification must be made to the analysis of life space. In considering the various categories above, we have had in mind men and women in full-time employment. Certain modifications to the scheme are necessary if it is to describe the lives of other groups. In assuming that all adults work (that is, are engaged in a full-time paid occupation) we should be right in about 60 per cent of cases. But an analysis of life space based on this majority would be incomplete if it could not be amended to take account of the large minority who do not have full-time jobs. Although there are some small minorities of the non-employed such as prisoners and the 'idle rich', the largest groups are housewives, the unemployed and the retired, and the situation of these groups will be considered in more detail in Chapter 6. Initially, however, some remarks on the significance of constraint and freedom in the lives of these three groups may be in order.

The life of the housewife tends to be restricted at both ends of the constraint–freedom scale. There is for her no real difference between work and work obligations, and the responsibilities of the household (particularly if she is a mother) must often restrict the range of her leisure activities, even though her 'free time' may be greater than that of her employed sister. The proportion of her time devoted to non-work obligations is correspondingly inflated. It is interesting to note that time budgets collected in ten countries show that non-employed women more often combine primary and secondary activities in the same space of time than do either employed men or women. In this sense at least, the lives of housewives may be fuller than those of other people.

The unemployed constitute another category whose lives show a contraction of the normal range between constraint and freedom. Many people who are unemployed develop after a time a feeling of being useless, and may be driven to occupy themselves with trivial tasks and time-filling routines. They lose the companionship and social support of workmates. Lack of money produces a restriction on the range of leisure activities which they can engage in, thus narrowing the range of life experience from the leisure end as well as the work end.

Finally, people who have retired from employment are in a somewhat similar position to the unemployed. Both groups have lost the contrast, or at least the change of pace, between work and leisure that characterises the lives of the employed. But for the retired the absence of employment is permanent rather than temporary. Whereas unemployed people (except those approaching retirement age) may normally expect to find jobs in the future, the change of status for the retired is a prospect that faces them for the rest of their lives. For better or worse, they are launched on a life free from work, or at least free from employment. Whether this amounts to a life of leisure we shall examine in Chapter 6.

2

Work and Leisure in History and Other Societies

When discussing the problems of work and leisure we tend to take for granted the circumstances and conditions of modern industrial societies. But to understand the real range of social behaviour in these spheres we need to take a wider historical and anthropological look at work and leisure. In this chapter I shall first review the various meanings that work has had through the ages, then trace the historical development of the concept and practice of leisure, and finally compare the different ways in which work and leisure have been (and still are) related in societies other than modern industrial ones.

Historical Meanings of Work

Work, writes Marshall McLuhan (1964), does not exist in a non-literate world: it begins with the division of labour and the specialisation of functions and tasks in sedentary, agricultural communities. Obviously he is taking a rather narrow view of work. A more defensible statement is that work (in its widest sense, including labour) is a basic condition of the existence and continuation of human life – it is independent of any particular form of society. This does not, of course, apply to all forms of work. Only some forms are necessary for the production and reproduction of the means of life, others may be required in the development and preservation of particular types of social institution, while yet others result in the production of relatively inessential goods and services. The development of civilisation corresponds in one sense to the diversity of employments in which men engage and to the expansion of the area of goods and services which are regarded as necessities. At different stages of social development, societies have various ways of defining the scope of human work in terms of the goods or services required. But there is a deeper meaning of work as itself a value that is at least partly independent of its product.

It is only for the last few decades that we have any reasonably objective documentation of the meaning of work for the mass of people. Earlier surveys, such as Henry Mayhew's classic *London Labour and the London Poor*, which covered material conditions, did not extend to attitudes to those conditions. Thus we have little or no evidence of how 'the common man' conceived of work in earlier times. The clues that we have to the various historical meanings of work must be gained from philosophical and religious writers and refer to the ideal of work held by an elite. For the rest, the 'problem' of the meaning of work did not exist. For most of history men have *been* what they *did*: a man's work provided him with an identity that was recognised both by others and by himself. It is also worth remembering that to ask men in economically undeveloped traditional societies why they work is similar to asking them why they try to stay alive.

To the ancient Greeks, in whose society mechanical labour was done by slaves, work was a curse and nothing else (Tilgher, 1931). It was coloured with that sense of a heavy burdensome task which we feel in the words fatigue, travail, burden. The Greeks regarded as drudgery physical work of every sort. Work was seen as brutalising the mind, making man unfit for thinking of truth or for practising virtue; it was a necessary material evil which the visionary elite should avoid. Agriculture was grudgingly accepted as not unworthy of a citizen, because it brought independence, but free artisans and craftsmen were scorned as hardly better than slaves.

Like the Greeks, the Hebrews thought of work as a painful necessity, but added the belief that it was a product of original sin. It was accepted as expiation through which man might atone for the sin of his ancestors and co-operate with God in the world's salvation. Not only intellectual but also manual work thus acquired dignity and value. Primitive Christianity followed the Jewish tradition in regarding work as punishment for original sin, but added a positive function: work is necessary above all in order to share what is produced with one's needy brothers. But no intrinsic value was recognised in labour – it was still only a means to a worthy end. Early Catholicism did something to dignify labour, but mainly of the religious and intellectual kind. Pure contemplation was placed above even intellectual monastery work. In medieval Europe heretical sects preached work not because it is good but because they believed it painful, humiliating, 'a scourge for the pride of the flesh'. As the church drew closer to accepting worldly standards, it granted fuller justice to labour and its fruits. St Thomas Aquinas drew up a hierarchy of professions and trades, ranking agriculture first, then the handicrafts, and commerce last. But although work then appeared as a natural right and duty, it was still regarded as preferable to pray and contemplate God.

Protestantism was the force that established work in the modern mind as 'the base and key of life'. In Luther's teachings work was still natural to fallen man, but all who could work should do so. With the idea that the best way to serve God was to do most perfectly the work of one's profession, Luther swept away the distinction between religious piety and worldly activity; profession became 'calling' and work was valued as a religious path to salvation.

Calvin developed these ideas further with his concept of predestination. Only a small part of mankind shall know everlasting life; idleness and luxury are deadly sins, and dislike of work is a sign that 'election' is doubtful. All men, even the rich, must work because it is the will of God. But they must not lust after the fruits of their labour. From this paradox – the command to ceaseless effort, to ceaseless renunciation of the fruits of effort – the motive power and ideological justification of modern business derives. Unlike Luther, Calvin considered it no virtue to stay in the class or profession to which one is born. It is the duty of everyone to seek out the profession which will bring him, and hence society, the greatest return. Work is thus freed from the hampering ideas of caste and becomes mobile and rationalised. Puritanism, developing out of Calvinism, went further yet recalled the early Christian tradition; work was valued not for love of money or pleasure but as a means whereby 'more benediction may fall upon the next needy person'. But the main legacy of Calvinism arises from its paradoxical command to deny the world but live in the world, to work hard to accumulate wealth but not to spend it on oneself. This is the foundation of the nineteenth-century cult of work for the sake of work, and the abhorrence of idleness and pleasure.

However, the nineteenth century also brought a reaction to these ideas about the religious motivation of work. Since the Renaissance some men had held the view that creative work could be a joy in itself. The early Utopians had taken an essentially non-religious view of the role of work in man's life. Campanella, in his *City of the Sun*, made all members of society workers who were joyful because each had work suitable to his character and which he need do for only four hours a day. In Thomas More's *Utopia* the working day is six hours, but all men take their turn at all kinds of work. The nineteenth-century socialists, contemporaries and followers of Marx and Engels, tended to be critical of the 'idealistic' implications of Utopianism, but held views on work which were broadly similar. Morelly believed that

man is a naturally active being who does not in the least dislike work as such, but only when it is monotonous and lasts too long. If men seem to hate work that is only because arbitrary institutions have given part of mankind a perpetual holiday called prosperity, and sentenced the rest to hard labour for life.

The Marxist socialists formulated, a century or more ago, basic predictions which their descendants continue to hold today. When production is carried on solely for use and not for profit, when men are no longer compelled to work at unpleasant or boring jobs just to earn a living, they will have more zeal for work, which will be done less by routine and more by reason. It will be better organised and require less time for a greater output. Workers will have leisure time for a freer and more truly human life.

Modern meanings attached to work are still influenced by some of the older conceptions, as we shall see in the next chapter. It is also worth drawing attention to another traditional way of looking at work – that common to most primitive communities still existing today. There are some parts of the world that do not have a wage system in which so much reward is given for so much labour or labour time, and in these communities it is possible to see, perhaps more clearly than in our own society, that work has functions other than economic ones. Participation in work is often undertaken as a duty towards the person who wants the work done, rather than for the material gain that can be expected from him. But work for its own sake is not regarded as a duty. This meaning of work as duty to others recalls the early Christian tradition but without its connotation as punishment for original sin.

Historical Development of Leisure

We tend to think of leisure as a product of modern civilisation, and in a sense this is true. During the last hundred years or so we have moved from a typical seventy-hour to roughly a forty-hour average working week. But taking a longer historical view we see that the gain in leisure with economic growth has been exaggerated. Estimates of annual and lifetime leisure suggest that the skilled urban worker today may only have regained the position of his thirteenth-century counterpart (Wilensky, 1960). This is because in medieval times about one day in three was a holiday of some kind. In the perspective of several centuries, the amount of time spent at work, at first relatively low, increased during the Industrial Revolution, and is only now decreasing to something like its earlier level.

Taking an even longer time perspective, we can see that during most of the seven or eight millennia of civilisation the majority of men and women have had to work hard to sustain themselves and their families. Tradition inhibited spontaneous activities, though 'free time' was not always limited: according to Sahlins (1972), 'subsistence economies' do not dedicate more than three or four hours a day to material necessities. The life of the peasant (and it must be remembered that the majority of mankind are still peasants) is a continuous round of labour, but not necessarily more hours in total than for employees in industrial societies. In the countries affected by the Hebrew tradition there is the Sabbath, but that is not so much a day of leisure as a day of ceremonial inactivity, a day of restraint. It was only at the centres where wealth accumulated or where a strong element of nomadism remained that holy days lost their severity and became holidays.

Among early civilisations the Greek and Roman cities featured leisure in something like the modern sense, though only for a privileged elite (Martin and Norman, 1970). The leisured class in these societies was a minority and it had a slave or lower class to perform its routine work. To the Greeks, leisure was concerned with those activities that were worthy of a free man, activities which we might today call 'culture'. Politics, debate, philosophy, art, ritual, and athletic contests were activities worthy of a free man because they expressed the moral core of a style of life. The Greek word for leisure, *schole*, meant spare time, leisure, school. Unlike the modern conception of leisure as time saved from work, *schole* was a conscious abstention from all activities connected with merely being alive, consuming activities no less than producing. Nothing illustrates better the difference between Greek values and those prevailing in modern industrial society than their word for the work of a gentleman. They could express it only negatively as having no leisure – *ascholia*.

Thorstein Veblen (1925) went back further to the barbarian stage of social development to find the origins of his 'theory of the leisure class':

> During the predatory culture labour comes to be associated in men's habits of thought with weakness and subjection to a master. It is therefore a mark of inferiority, and therefore comes to be accounted unworthy of man in his best estate. By virtue of this tradition labour is felt to be debasing, and this tradition has never died out. (pp. 41–2)

To gain esteem it is not sufficient merely to possess wealth or power – it must be put in evidence. This is achieved partly by conspicuous abstention from labour. The leisurely life of a ruling class is thus a means of its gaining the respect of others.

In pre-industrial societies the majority of people had leisure only in the sense of mere rest from toil and of participation in stereotyped ceremonies. This was not conscious leisure, or the result of an exercise of individual choice, but part of the regular pattern of living. The same applies to many non-industrial societies today. In his study of the Ecuadorean Indians, Salz (1955) notes that all their time is used, if not in work, then in other 'structured activities'. Such festive occasions as weddings, christenings, birthdays and fiestas are common, and seem to have an obligatory character as well as serving as leisure activities. They are what Dumazedier calls semi-leisure and take the place of individually pursued leisure.

In the history of humanity, the idea of work in the modern sense is comparatively recent. Rhee (1968) makes this point forcibly by means of a time scale: 'if we think of humanity as having existed for one day, the notion of work as an activity in contrast to other human activities emerged only in the last quarter of an hour'. The experience of employment is, of course, an even more recent phenomenon, occupying less than a minute of humanity's day. The same applies to the concept of leisure as a separate part of life.

Work and Leisure in Non-Industrial Societies

We have seen that 'work' in the early civilisations was divisible roughly according to the distinction between labour and work made by Arendt. Labour meant providing the necessities of life; it symbolised man's dependence on nature and accordingly was performed by a class of labourers or by slaves. Work, in Arendt's sense, was effort of a different kind, creative, of the spirit, performed by free men and citizens. Between work of this latter kind and leisure there could logically be no dividing line, as Heckscher (1963) points out.

> Afterwards there was need for rest; there was need for re-creation in the exact sense of reconstituting the faculties for the pursuits of another day. But the idea that there could be a meaningful way of life, separate from the giving of themselves voluntarily to what they deemed significant and delightful, did not occur to the men of these earlier, classic periods. (p. 161)

Under pre-literate conditions, too, the line between labour and leisure is not sharply drawn. In so far as there is no separate 'leisure class', the separation of productive activities into work and labour is also less obvious than in more civilised societies. Primitive people do not make the clear distinction between work and leisure that we tend to make in modern society (Kraus, 1978). The orientation of life is towards long periods of work interspersed with occasional periods of intense expenditure of energy. Wax (1958) remarks on this fusion of work and leisure: 'I do not believe that any Bushman could tell us – or would be interested in telling us – which part of [his] activity was work and which was play.' Life in primitive societies follows a predetermined pattern in which work and non-work are inextricably confused. In these societies there are no clearly defined periods of leisure as such, but economic activities, like hunting or market-going, obviously have their recreational aspects, as do singing and telling stories at work. Though there are things done for enjoyment and recreation, the idea of time being set aside for this purpose is unfamiliar.

Work in co-operation is a frequent aspect of primitive economic life. The stimulus given by work accompanied by songs and jokes lightens drudgery and gives it some tinge of recreation. Ashton (1967) describes the co-operative work-parties (*matsema*) which are a feature of all phases of agricultural work among the Basuto:

> These are gay, sociable affairs comprising about 10–50 participants of both sexes . . . These *matsema* are useful though not very efficient. They assemble in the morning about 9 o'clock and work, with frequent breaks for light refreshment, until about 3 or 4 o'clock in the afternoon, to the accompaniment of ceaseless chatter and singing. (p. 131)

If labour is seen merely as a factor in production then this kind of behaviour is 'inefficient'. But the point is that it is useful to the people involved, that is, it is a preferred pattern. Work has its own psychological gains and losses, and it is no simple matter to decide the ways in which these balance up to provide a resultant of satisfaction or deprivation.

However, some pre-industrial societies do make a distinction between work and leisure, in a way that is quite close to the contemporary, although not to the traditional, Western pattern. Thus the lives of the Baluchi of Western Pakistan are divided into a sphere of duty or obligation necessary for life in civil society and an area which they call the sphere of one's own will (Wax, 1958). They seem to regard the latter as being a sphere of freedom and distraction from the workaday world. But whereas the Western tradition is to see the workaday world as the foundation of existence, the Baluchi invert the emphasis. For them – as indeed for growing numbers of people in Western society today – the world of their own will is the cherished area, the one in which they spend their energy and imagination and ingenuity.

At one point in its history one relatively sophisticated culture made such a sharp distinction between work and sacred activities that a combination of the two was viewed as blasphemous. This was the rigorously enforced 'leisure' of the pious medieval Jew who, when engaged in sacred matters, avoided anything remotely connected with work. But though it was the polar opposite of practical mundane activity, Judaic piety was by no means the same as play or free time. Indeed, it entailed more work and more trouble than any of the stringent, time-consuming activities of the secular world.

One of the biggest differences in the meaning of leisure is that between urban and rural communities. Leisure in agricultural societies is structured by the rhythm of necessary daily tasks and of the seasons, and is embedded in life rather than a separate part of it. Before the Industrial Revolution work and leisure were structured around rural events, for example, when the harvest had to be taken in people worked long hours, and in winter when daylight was short they worked less (Bacon, 1972b). The point is also illustrated by the reaction of Texan homesteaders to the possibility of inheriting a large fortune. Some thought they would take time off to go hunting and fishing, but no one considered complete leisure a possible way of life (Vogt, 1955).

Although Victorian Britain was in some ways already an advanced industrial society, it also constituted an interim period between a society based largely on rural communities and the twentieth-century refinements of industrialised, mass-consumer society. The distinction between work and leisure, as it evolved at that time, was neither absolute nor was it the same for each individual (Lowerson and Myerscough, 1977). Work and leisure intermingled in the life of the workshop where traditional craft practices laid down the ritual patterns of celebration and good fellowship (Bailey, 1978). But for those workers in industries where the machine or a new work ethic had come to dominate, custom was ceasing to have much value. At the same time, the entrepreneurs of entertainment were beginning to see new commercial possibilities in a world where leisure was both more regular and more separate from work (Cunningham, 1980).

What are the general conclusions to be drawn from studies of work and leisure in types of society other than our own? First, work seems usually to have been identified with the constraint of labour, though the forms that this constraint has taken – as an obstacle to 'higher things', as a purgative, or as social duty – are today absent or muted themes when compared with the economic constraint to earn a living. Secondly, sandwiched between the earlier religious views of work and the nineteenth-century Protestant cult of work for the sake of work, there was the Renaissance view of work as creative, intrinsically satisfying activity. Thirdly, the absence of a sharp demarcation between work and leisure in most pre-literate and rural societies has two aspects: the more leisurely character of work, but the greater importance of non-work obligations as compared with the type of leisure most often experienced in modern industrial societies. And lastly, the degree to which work and leisure are experienced, in fact and in ideology, as separate parts of life seems to be related to the degree to which the society itself is stratified, work being the lot of the masses and leisure that of the elite.

What do these conclusions imply for the future of work and leisure in our own society? If technological advances mean that, in the future, a smaller proportion of our time (or the time of a smaller proportion of people) must be devoted to earning a living, it is quite possible that some of the older meanings of work will reassert themselves. For most people leisure is now definitely marked off from work, but historically this may be seen as a pleasure-seeking reaction to a philosophy of work for the sake of work. There is no reason to suppose that this reaction will go on for ever. Perhaps the biggest question mark hangs over the future of the class system. Hitherto there have been 'working classes' and 'leisure classes' (that is, privileged classes of one kind or another). Today, although the social system is still based on private property with consequent inequality and privilege, there are working people who are also people of leisure – mass leisure. So those who believe in elites may have to pin their faith on differences in the *style* of both work and leisure rather than on the exclusive class participation in one or the other. On the other hand, those who favour social equality will seek to make work a more rewarding experience for the mass of people and to narrow the gap in opportunities between the more and the less privileged with respect to leisure experiences.

3

What Does Work Mean Today?

In this chapter I shall look at the different ways in which men and women earn their living in our society and the different meanings that work has for them. The various sources of satisfaction and dissatisfaction that people have in their work tell us something about how well or how badly the content and organisation of the work is suited to their needs. The different meanings that people tend to attach to work according to the type of job they do, and the widespread feeling of alienation from work, are other aspects that merit attention. Finally, I return to the important point made in Chapter 1 that employment is not the whole of work, and we see that much of the dissatisfaction and lack of meaning that is today attributed to 'work' rightly belongs only to employment.

Work Satisfaction

The statements that follow are based on data from two sources: (1) surveys carried out by various social researchers, including myself, and (2) case studies from the *New Left Review*'s two volumes of *Work: Twenty Personal Accounts* (Fraser, 1968–9). It is hoped that this mixture of the statistically respectable and the humanly interesting will be more acceptable than either source alone.

Many occupations have been the subject of work satisfaction studies, though factory and office work have predominated. Among skilled factory workers and craftsmen intrinsic satisfaction with the work itself is frequently found, especially when the job involves completion of a whole product. Assembly-line workers attach more importance to being able to control to some extent the pace and methods of their work. Variety of operations is a source of satisfaction to both factory and office workers, and among the latter the friendliness of the working group is often mentioned (particularly by women). In comparing proportions of satisfied workers in different occupations, there seem to be separate scales for manual and non-manual jobs, with more satisfaction found at the higher levels of skill in each group. Professional workers are the most satisfied, and semi-skilled and unskilled manual workers least so.

Of 'special situation' factors which influence work satisfaction, social interaction seems to be most important. Insecurity in a job, even when accompanied by good objective conditions, adversely affects satisfaction. Autonomy in the work situation – freedom to make decisions and take responsibilities – is positively related to satisfaction. If three individuals are engaged on the same work with mates doing respectively a better, worse, or the same job, the first is likely to show least job enjoyment. Permissive supervision and leadership, and being consulted in advance about changes in work processes, are conducive to satisfaction. In general, jobs which involve dealing with people provide more satisfaction than those which do not.

The above is a brief summary of some of the main findings from surveys of work satisfaction. These findings give us some idea of the sources of satisfaction and the features of jobs which produce satisfaction, but we need the benefit of more personal accounts to understand the full richness – and also the relative poverty – of people's working lives. If we put these personal accounts within a framework then we can preserve both a personal approach and a systematic one: we understand people more fully and we understand society more fully.

Let us first consider some of the main themes which emerge from the statements of men and women about what makes work satisfying to them.

(1) *Creating something.* This is compounded of a feeling that one has put something of oneself into a product and a deep sense of pleasure in the act of creation itself. It is perhaps the most common of all the expressed feelings of satisfaction and felt by the widest range of workers, both manual and non-manual. Referring to steelmaking in the early years of the present century, a steelman writes that 'every pot of steel was an act of creation. It was something derived from the absorbed attention of dedicated men'. An accountant describes his work partly as 'an act of creation, i.e. if the thing is right there is a form about it, a kind of beauty which comes from its structure; it exists that way because it has been made from the right bits and pieces'. Sometimes the feeling of creating something is linked to how the product fits into the scheme of things. Thus toolmaking 'was obviously a source of much ego-contentment and status. Each man made a complete tool, jig or punch and die by himself'. Even a product which is in fact created by a number of people can give satisfaction to the one who can feel that it is really 'his'. A journalist, otherwise indifferent to his work, writes that 'for the time it took me to re-read one of "my" stories in the papers next day, I too felt the satisfaction of having created'.

(2) *Using skill*. This is often associated with creating something, but it lays more emphasis on what the work does for the person rather than the product. Again, the use of skill cuts across the manual/non-manual division of work. 'The skilled worker has to work out, from drawings, the best method of doing the particular job; he has to set his own machine, he has to get the necessary tools out of the stores, he has to grind his own tools, and so on. Using his ingenuity and his skill, the worker is constantly made aware of his active and valuable role in the productive process.' The bricklayer finding 'a certain joy in being able to do something competently with one's hands and in using muscular force with common sense to overcome obstacles' and the computer programmer delighting in the scope his job has for technical ingenuity are other examples of the different ways in which satisfaction can be gained from the use of skills.

(3) *Working wholeheartedly*. Various restrictions on full productive effort by workers (attempting to beat the rate-fixer or time-study man, working to rule, go-slows, and so on) are common in industry today. But there is no evidence that these are preferred patterns of working and they mostly exist in the battle to get more money. More enlightened management policies than most existing ones could surely turn to better account the knowledge that most people enjoy working wholeheartedly provided that they do not feel that they lose financially by doing so. A salesman expresses this idea clearly and simply: 'Like most people, I enjoy working wholeheartedly when I work.' A bricklayer says that 'the jobs I have enjoyed most are those where I have worked the hardest'. A slight variation of this theme is the fact that few people like to turn out substandard work.

(4) *Using initiative and having responsibility*. This includes a feeling of freedom to take decisions and a certain independence of authority in the sense of people telling you what to do. To some extent the satisfaction derived from a job having these characteristics is a matter of personality and upbringing. Someone who has been raised and educated in the tradition of conformity and subservience to authority may not wish to use his initiative or have responsibility in his job. But it seems that most people value the opportunity to think and act in their work as responsible and relatively autonomous individuals. Even those workers who are 'not paid to think' often find it helps the job to go well if they do. A machine minder will replace the broken part of a machine without calling the supervisor because 'it's quicker and more interesting to do it yourself'. Another aspect of responsibility is well expressed by the doctor's secretary who found that 'one of the chief attractions of the job for me is the feeling of being in charge, feeling that I matter . . . I would certainly be missed if I left'.

(5) *Mixing with people.* This is an outstanding source of satisfaction to people whose work involves dealing with customers or clients. The attraction may lie in the variety of people one meets, the feeling of being able to help or teach others, the use of independent judgement as in casework, or simply the pleasure derived from social contact. A teacher writes that his job is 'concerned with growing and developing individuals who are never predictable, and so provide a variety of experience which is always stimulating'. Those whose work brings them into regular contact with other people may not always feel (as does one minister) 'increasingly refreshed and healed by personal encounter', but at least they will mostly agree with the doctor's secretary that 'it is much more interesting to follow cases than costs'.

(6) *Working with people who know their job.* The 'human relations' school of industrial sociology stresses how important it is to have good communication between managers and workers and that it helps if managers show a friendly and interested approach towards their workers. However, if this is merely used as a technique, people tend to 'see through it'. A deeper respect seems to be accorded bosses who really know their job. Among the things that one town planner looks for in a job is the opportunity 'to work for people who know how to get a job done and who are not afraid or ashamed to be seen to be responsible'. Mutual respect is looked for; in the words of a steelman, 'to know that a manager knew his job and that he respected one reciprocally was a good thing all round, good for the metal, good for the melter, and good for the manager'.

So far I have described some of the positive satisfactions that people gain from their work. What can be said of the things that cause dissatisfaction? Obviously some of these are simply the opposite of the things discussed above – not being able to create anything, using no skill, and so on. But the emphases are rather different. Again, drawing on a number of Fraser's accounts, we can see several themes of dissatisfaction.

(1) *Doing repetitive work.* This produces a feeling of never really achieving anything and of failing to use one's human faculties. It has long been recognised as a problem in industry, and attempts to ameliorate it include shifting workers from one job to another as frequently as possible (job rotation). The full effect of repetitive work on human beings is incalculable, but we have the evidence of a few articulate victims. 'Nothing is gained from the work itself – it has nothing to offer . . . Either one job is followed by another which is equally boring, or the same job goes on for ever: particles of production that stretch into an age of inconsequence. There is never a sense of fulfilment.' Sometimes fully mechanical work may be preferred to work which requires a little attention because it enables the person to

absent himself mentally from the job. Thus a housewife complains of 'the sameness of jobs that require perhaps less than a quarter of one's mental awareness, while leaving the rest incapable of being occupied elsewhere'.

(2) *Making only a small part of something.* Long ago Karl Marx drew attention to what he called the excessive division of labour under capitalism: the forcing of men into a specialisation of function that becomes more and more narrow and less and less inclusive of their various potentials. Despite some attempts to give people more of a whole job to do (job enlargement) there is still plenty of work that in effect makes the worker, in Marx's phrase, an appendage to a machine. One operative expresses the view that 'the worker's role is becoming more and more that of an onlooker and less that of a participant . . . The loss of dignity and restriction of talent compatible with modern factory life cause a lack of quality in the factory worker'. To a toolmaker, 'the normal lot of the industrial worker is a very unsatisfactory work experience of performing a fragmented task under conditions he can only marginally control'. These observations suggest that fragmented tasks not only mean less participation by the worker in the total work process but also affect his whole way of life and restrict his personal development.

(3) *Doing useless tasks.* It can be argued that any work for which someone is prepared to pay or to authorise payment presumably has a use. But this ignores the extent to which the whole present system of production and distribution has become remote from direct personal needs as it has become 'mass'. Much of the growth in the service occupations has to do with protecting property. A nightwatchman describes his workgroup as 'a hive of men guarding the sleep of capital. Producing nothing, this labour exists to make nothing happen, its aim is emptiness'. Another type of task commonly felt to be useless is form-filling. In offices, factories, schools and hospitals the amount of paperwork is steadily increasing. The occupations it provides are seldom satisfying to the people concerned. Writing about himself and his fellows, a clerk remarks that 'unlike even the humblest worker on a production line, he doesn't produce *anything*. He battles with phantoms, abstracts: runs in a paper chase that goes on year after year, and seems utterly pointless'.

(4) *Feeling a sense of insecurity.* The recurrent economic difficulties of the country, combined with technological and organisational changes in employing organisations, have resulted in an increase in unemployment and redundancy. This, in turn, has led to mounting fears about the security of jobs. As previously noted, a feeling of insecurity seems to spill over into dissatisfaction with many other aspects of a job. Few people seem able to analyse their feelings of

insecurity but many of them mention it in talking about their work. 'There is a general feeling of frustration, a feeling that life has little purpose in such insecure conditions where everyone is threatened with the loss of his job' (warehouseman). Sometimes the loss of a job is at least partly looked forward to. 'You feel dispensable, interim: automation will take the job over one day, the sooner the better' (clerk).

(5) *Being too closely supervised.* Much has been learned by industrial researchers about the most appropriate and acceptable forms of supervision, but few of the lessons seem to have been learned by management. Office workers are more often the victims of inhuman supervisory systems than are factory workers. The clerk quoted above describes the worst kinds of supervision, 'those that have you lined up in rows facing the front, with the eagle eye on you and no excuse for moving at all'. In social work and teaching the grievances concerning supervision take a rather different form. A child care officer explains how the 'hierarchy' is a drag on growth and change: 'What each of us needed in the job was the awareness to know what people were really saying, or trying to say, and to then decide how we could help them. To be assigned a role in a hierarchy contributed nothing to that.' Similarly a teacher complains that the bureaucratic structure of the school means that the school governors and senior staff 'wish to supervise the minutest details of the projects they organise'.

The themes of satisfaction and dissatisfaction discussed above cover many aspects of the jobs that most people do today. Much that could be changed and improved seems to be taken for granted or accepted with resignation. Perhaps the most remarkable thing about the findings in general is the large gap they show between the most and the least rewarding kinds and conditions of work – a gap that cannot be entirely justified by differences in the abilities and potentialities of the individuals in the different kinds of job.

Meanings of Work

The concept of 'meaning' overlaps that of satisfaction (or dissatisfaction). When someone says that he finds his work satisfying because it is, for example, creative, this is a way of saying that the work has meaning for him, that he can see the purpose for which it is done and that he agrees with this purpose. On the other hand, a worker may be dissatisfied with his job because he feels it to be 'meaningless' in the sense of not understanding where his contribution fits into the whole, or even (in the case of highly fragmented work) not knowing what that contribution is. Strictly speaking, of course, any kind of work must mean something, even if it is nothing more than a way of earning a living.

A number of academic studies have sought to define various meanings of work held by people in different occupations and work situations. Weiss and Kahn (1960) found that over three-quarters of their respondents defined work either as activity which was necessary though not enjoyed or as activity which was scheduled or paid for. The first definition was associated with occupations which permit some autonomy (professionals and salespeople) and the second with occupations with neither social standing nor autonomy (factory workers and labourers). Friedmann and Havighurst (1954) compared the meaning of work to five occupational groups. The workers of lower skill and socioeconomic status were more likely to see their work as having no other meaning than that of earning money. Coal miners had a more personal sense than steelworkers of struggling against their environment and expressed feelings of accomplishment and pride at having conquered it. Skilled craftsmen showed a very high degree of emphasis on work as a source of self-respect and the respect of others. All of the salespeople surveyed recognised some meaning in their work beyond earning a living, and the most popular meanings were 'something to do and think about' and sociability and friendship. Finally, the physicians were found to stress most the public service aspect of their jobs.

The method used by Morse and Weiss (1955) to study the meaning of work was to ask people whether they would continue working if they inherited enough money to live comfortably without working. They concluded that, to those in middle-class occupations, work means having something interesting to do, having a chance to accomplish things and to contribute, while those in working-class occupations view work as synonymous with activity. These differences in work meanings correspond to differences in the content of the jobs. The content of professional, managerial and sales jobs concerns symbols and the handling of cases, and so a life without such work would be less purposeful, stimulating and challenging. Working-class occupations emphasise working with tools and machines, and the individual is oriented to the effort rather than to the end-product – life without such work would mean life without anything to do.

A threefold division of the meaning of work less fragmented than that of Friedmann and Havighurst but not so simplified as that of Morse and Weiss is suggested by Peter Berger (1964):

First, there is work that still provides an occasion for primary self-identification and self-commitment of the individual – for his 'fulfilment', if one prefers. *Thirdly*, there is work that is apprehended as a direct threat to self-identification, an indignity, an oppression. And

secondly, between these two poles, is work that is neither fulfilment nor oppression, a sort of gray, neutral region in which one
neither rejoices nor suffers, but with which one puts up with more
or less grace for the sake of other things that are supposed to be
important . . . In the first category, of course, are to be placed most
so-called professions and the upper-echelon positions in the
various bureaucratic apparatuses. In the third category continue to
remain many of the unskilled occupations 'in the basement' of
the industrial system. And in between, in the second category, is
to be found the bulk of both white-collar and blue-collar work.
(pp. 218–19)

The findings of the academic studies and generalisations made by
Berger do seem to fit in reasonably well with many of the personal
accounts quoted in the previous section. The conclusions of the
studies are couched in the language used by the researchers themselves, and reveal a certain amount of middle-class bias. Undoubtedly
there are broad differences in the meanings attached to work, but we
must beware of too-sweeping generalisations. Not all middle-class
and professional occupations are 'fulfilling' to their holders, although
a desire to achieve status or success may lead to exaggerated claims
about the most trivial and socially useless occupations. On the other
hand, the poor economic and social rewards of many so-called
working-class occupations should not obscure their real value both to
society and to the workers themselves.

The meaning of work varies with three main factors: type of occupation (skills used), industry (use to which the skills are put) and status
(position in the employing organisation or in society). In many cases
the content of the work will vary with employment status, but even
where the content of the work is the same or very similar work
attitudes may vary according to status. Thus laboratory workers were
found to differ in their work values according to whether they were
'professionals' or 'technicians', even though both groups had roughly
the same kind of tasks (Boggs, 1963). The professionals were far more
likely to say that the kind of work they did was the most important
thing about a life's work, while the technicians more often said that
security or pay was the most important thing.

A notable difference in status, or *social* position in society, is perhaps
better understood as a difference in class, or *economic* position in
society: that between workers and capitalists. The term 'capitalist' has
pejorative overtones, but as applied to those persons who possess
capital the return on which enables them to live without the necessity
of being employed it has a reasonably precise meaning. The term
'employer' can, in fact, be a misleading antonym of 'employee' if it

denotes a person who hires and fires employees, since that person, no less than those he hires and fires, is usually an employee of an organisation owned by shareholders or controlled by the state or other public authority. There is nothing to stop a capitalist being an employee, though naturally he will usually choose to be an employee at a high-status level appropriate to his economic position.

Those highly paid employees at managerial level who approach or are at the economic position of capitalists are able, because of their stronger bargaining position, to obtain favourable terms of employment, often including the ability to determine their own working hours. Their work, though more demanding, is usually intrinsically more interesting, partly because they make decisions instead of having to conform to other people's decisions. In short, we may divide people into three broad groups with regard to work experience: the capitalists, who have no need of employment but may work if they wish (minimum constraint); the managers, who are employed on favourable terms (medium constraint); and the mass of employees, who are compelled to work for a living (maximum constraint). Inevitably, work must mean different things to these three groups.

Alienation from Work

The theme of alienation from work is widely used to describe the disengagement of self from the occupational role. As some of the personal accounts showed, workers tend to become frustrated by the lack of meaning in the tasks allotted to them and by the impersonality of their role in the work organisation. Such workers are virtually forced to turn to non-work life for a sense of values and identity: 'I only work here, but if you want to know me as I really am, come to my home and meet my family.' Alienation can also take subtler forms among professionals and executives, for whom it may be fashionable to be cynical about one's work but quite 'satisfied' with one's job. Experience of alienation is not confined to a few special occupations, though it tends to be associated with certain characteristic work situations. In bureaucratic organisations it is apparent in the administration of people as if they were things. In an automated factory or office it takes the form of increasing the number of people who deal with the world through abstractions.

An important contribution to understanding the nature and correlates of alienation from work has been made by Robert Blauner (1964). In making a comparative analysis of four types of work situation, he seeks to show that alienation is a function of the type of industry in which people work. He analysed the dimensions of alienation as *powerlessness* (inability to control the work process), *meaninglessness* (inability to develop a sense of purpose connecting the job to the overall productive process), *isolation* (inability to belong to integrated industrial communities) and *self-estrangement* (failure to become involved in the activity of work as a mode of self-expression). The four types compared were the printing, textiles, automobile and chemical industries. The general picture was of a relative lack of alienation in craft printing, an increase in alienation in machine textiles, a further increase in the assembly-line automobile industry, but a reduction in the automated chemical industry to something like the level found in the printing industry.

Blauner's analysis has been criticised as resting too much on the type of industry as the determining factor in level of alienation (Eldridge, 1971). Also, Seeman (1967) has used his own research in Sweden to question some of the wider claims made concerning alienation, such as that it is correlated with lack of knowledge and lack of interest in political matters. There is no serious suggestion, however, that the basic theme of alienation is invalid or that its experience among at least some employees today is insignificant.

In industry generally there has in recent years been a levelling of the use of skill, and this seems likely to continue for some while yet. Both craftsmen and unskilled manual workers are steadily being replaced by operatives in semi-automated plants. It is claimed that as we move towards full automation work will become 'humanised' – the machines will do all the hard and routine work, leaving man free to plan and control (see Chapter 9). The difference between semi-automation and full automation may, from the worker's point of view, represent a reduction in the feeling of alienation from work. To that extent, technological change is to be encouraged for what it can do for people as well as for production. But not all production of goods and services is going to be automated, and the aim of making the experience of work more meaningful and less alienating stands in its own right.

Assuming resumed growth, after the present recession, in the social and welfare services there will be increasing numbers of jobs involving dealing with people, many of which will be regarded as more rewarding than most of the jobs which are disappearing. The implication of the growth of the 'leisure industries' for the meaning of work is not so clear. Unless there is a move away from commercialised amusement and towards do-it-yourself leisure pursuits, more people are likely to spend their working lives ministering to the leisure needs of others. At this stage we can only speculate on the effect that these changes will have on the meaning of work and the possible reduction of feelings of alienation.

Employment Is Not the Whole of Work

In line with common usage, and in order not to be pedantic, I have so far in this chapter used the word 'work' when strictly speaking the reference was to 'employment' or 'the job'. As noted in Chapter 1, work is a much wider concept than employment, although when we try to describe what work means for us today it is easy to think just of the content and conditions of the job that we have, that we would like, or that we have retired from. It is worth remembering that much economic activity takes place outside the formal economy altogether. Watts (1981) has noted six successively broader definitions of work:

(1) Formal paid employment within that sector of the economy which is directly concerned with wealth generation.
(2) Formal paid employment within large bureaucratic organisations.
(3) Formal paid employment within an organisation of any size (including small businesses).
(4) Economic activity within the formal economy.
(5) Economic activity rewarded by cash, whether within the formal economy or outside it.
(6) Any application of productive effort, such as the informal, self-service economy (see Gershuny, 1979; Heinze and Olk, 1982).

We also need to recognise that a good deal of what goes on 'at work' is *not* work at all – it is joking, horse-play, courtship, making friends, relieving boredom, and so on (Loizos, 1980). This 'leisure in work' depends on the extent to which the work situation allows opportunities for leisure-like behaviour. In some cases, for example, the British shipyard workers studied by Brown and his colleagues (1973), leisure activities such as exchanging stories and playing cards are an integral part of the work context: they are the cement of social relationships in work and the fabric of the occupational culture.

Employment is essentially a social relationship, not to be equated with the performance of work. As Pym (1979) remarks, it is important to distinguish between employment (the framework) and work (the act). So when we hear men and women complaining about their jobs they are not necessarily complaining about the work they do. They probably quite like their work, but hate the conditions under which they have to do it – the rules laid down by their employer about its timing and duration, and the poor pay they get for it. Books have been written with such titles as *The Flight from Work* (Palm, 1977) and *The Collapse of Work* (Jenkins and Sherman, 1979), but the flight and the collapse are from employment as we have known it rather than from the activity of work upon which all societies are built.

4

The Social and Individual Functions of Leisure

This is the age of increasing leisure, we are constantly told. But what kind of leisure? There are many ways of filling free time, ways which amount to a complex 'machinery of amusement', all the parts of which look different while probably performing in many cases the same function to the individual. And what of society itself – does it have an interest in the enjoyment of its leisure-seekers in any way comparable to its interest in the productivity of its workers? In a parallel exercise to that undertaken in the previous chapter we may look at the research findings on both the use of leisure time and the various meanings attached to leisure.

Leisure has functions in the life of an individual, and its experience by individuals and groups has functions for the society in which they live. We may consider first how leisure serves society. It does this in three main ways: (1) it helps people to learn how to play their part in society; (2) it helps them to achieve societal or collective aims; and (3) it helps the society to keep together (Gross, 1961). These functions apply to groups as well as to the wider society.

The word sociologists have for describing the process by which people learn how to play their part in society is 'socialisation'. It starts in childhood and continues into adult life as men and women have to learn how to cope with new situations and to fit in, more or less, with what is expected of them. Leisure in the form of play and story-telling is used as a technique for teaching young children and reconciling them to school work. Leisure in the form of horseplay and initiation ceremonies often helps to socialise young workers into their jobs.

The work essential to society is aided by the recreational function of leisure. After a certain point, work results in fatigue and often in boredom. With the intention of increasing productivity, some firms allow their workers more breaks than are strictly necessary for physiological purposes. Other firms encourage their workers to take 'wholesome recreation' off the job. In another sense, industry needs the 'consuming time' of workers as much as it needs their 'producing time'. Businessmen in the leisure industries are interested in making leisure serve economic purposes by encouraging people to buy leisure goods and to pay for leisure services. But a trade unionist, Mr E. S. Williams, made the following remarks in seconding a motion on reduced working hours and increased holidays:

> I would draw attention of the Congress to the need for our Movement to intensify its efforts among workpeople to ensure their full understanding of the need for adequate rest and leisure periods as essentials in the modern world of speed, speed and more speed. Intensification of effort over shorter working periods must be accompanied not only by longer rest and leisure periods but also by a full appreciation among our people of the need for them to use such leisure time in the pursuit of relaxation of their physical and mental processes which are of such importance in the modern industrial world. (Trades Union Congress, 1965)

It is not suggested that the views of Mr Williams are typical of trade unionists – his subordination of leisure to the needs of industry is more typical of the nineteenth-century cult of work than of the twentieth-century belief in leisure for its own sake. But old ideas die hard. Also under the heading of societal aims there is the motivation that leisure may provide for work. Acquiring expensive leisure objects such as boats or caravans may only be possible through extra work (normally either in the form of overtime or a second job) and the prospects of a life of total leisure may be the motive for certain types of gambling, such as the football pools.

Leisure may contribute to the integration of society by promoting solidarity. At work, people may behave in leisure-like ways, such as horsing around, which help them to feel a sense of belonging together. Play and sporting activities serve as focal points of group and community identification. Burawoy (1978) shows how games in workplaces are used to co-ordinate the apparent interests of workers and management. The very act of playing a game produces and reproduces consent to the rules and to the desirability of certain outcomes. Shop management (if not higher levels) becomes actively engaged in organising and facilitating games on the shop floor, particularly where they revolve around output.

A controversial question is the degree of organisation and planning that is acceptable in leisure activities. There is a paradox in seeking to plan for the use of what is supposed to be an uncommitted part of one's life. Since, however, the provision of leisure amenities and opportunities and the spread of ideas about how leisure time should be spent are largely functions of society, there is no guarantee that the absence of planning would increase the individual's choice of leisure opportunities. It also seems that the concept of 'choice' as an indispensable and realistic element in leisure may have been overstated (Parker, 1981; Corrigan, 1982).

The state's attitude to the use of leisure by its citizens reflects both its function as an integrative institution and the shared values of those it controls. All states in the modern industrial world exercise at least a minimal control over the leisure activities of individuals and groups. Some types of leisure behaviour or the provision of leisure facilities are defined as illegal and the 'leisure industries' are subject to the same general laws which control other enterprises. Beyond this, the attitude of the state to the use of leisure may vary both with its degree of economic development and with the political views dominant at different times. Countries such as China, having only recently embarked on the road to industrialisation, require their citizens to render additional service to the state in their free time, to engage in organised physical culture for greater work efficiency, and to use entertainment, music, literature and art to reinforce the state's economic objectives. In the Soviet Union, more open to influences from the West, there is conflict between the official intention to make leisure functional and the popular pressures to make it personal and hedonistic (Riordan, 1982). In the United States and in Britain government, as such, tends not to attempt to influence leisure activities, although the big business of commercialised leisure imposes its own standards of conformity. Against these controlling and conforming functions of the state and of commercial interests, leisure may also be seen as a source of social change by creating subcultures from which innovative forms of social behaviour can emerge (Wilson, 1980).

Turning now to the functions of leisure for the individual, these can be classified on the basis of observed behaviour. An important classification is that of Dumazedier (1967), who believes that leisure has three main functions of relaxation, entertainment and personal development. Relaxation provides recovery from fatigue and repairs the physical and nervous damage wrought by the tensions of daily pressures, particularly by those of the job. Entertainment provides relief from boredom – a break from daily routine. It contains a strong element of escape – realistic to the extent that it involves a change of place or style (trips, sports), and involving fantasy in the form of identification and projection (cinema, the novel, and so on).

Dumazedier's third function of leisure, personal development,

serves to liberate the individual from the daily automatism of thought and action. It permits a broader, readier social participation on the one hand, and on the other, a willing cultivation of the physical and mental self over and above utilitarian considerations of job or practical advancement. It may even lead to discovering new forms of voluntary learning for the rest of one's life and induce an entirely new kind of creative attitude. (p. 14)

Dumazedier observes that the three functions are interdependent and exist in varying degrees in everyone's life. They may coexist in a single leisure situation or may be exercised in turn.

Less comprehensive assessments of the roles of leisure may be fitted into the Dumazedier classification. One example is Faunce's (1959) statement that

leisure may be recuperative in the sense that time is spent relaxing from the job completed and preparing for the job forthcoming or it may be actively spent in the sense of physical or emotional involvement in an activity ... Leisure time may serve as a relief from boredom or as an escape from involvement.

Giddens's (1964) remarks on the two major psychological functions of play are slightly different ways of talking about relaxation and personal development: cathartic (dissipating tension accumulated in other spheres) and ego-expansion (satisfactions of achievement and self-realisation which are frustrated elsewhere).

The type of work experience does not enable us to predict actual leisure behaviour, but it does enable us to predict what sort of function may be served for the individual by leisure behaviour. Those who want excitement, as well as those who want quiet, may only be searching for compensations for conditions in the kind of working life they have. For example, excitement may be sought in leisure because most of one's working life is dull; and the duller it is, the cruder the excitement that is satisfying. In the preface to a study of pigeon cultivation among French miners, Friedmann (1960) pointed out that leisure does more than merely offer a compensation for the technique of work. It brings professional compensations for work with a limited horizon, emotional compensations for the crudity of social relations in a mass of people, and social compensations through the success which this leisure-time activity can provide. After quoting this study, Dumazedier and Latouche (1962) observe that, far from being a compensation, leisure is more often only an extension of occupational life. They refer to a study by Louchet showing that there is a tendency for the most frustrating leisure to be associated with the most frustrating work.

Although certain patterns of leisure behaviour may be observed, and its functions for individuals imputed, it would be unwise to imagine that our present knowledge is other than sketchy. As Glyptis

(1981) reminds us, we do not know whether people perceive of leisure at all, and if they do, whether they define it in terms of activities, times, places, companions, or states of mind. There is also the problem that what is leisure to one person is definitely not leisure to another. Thus, for some of the people studied by Glyptis, personal and child care, home and car maintenance and gardening were undertaken as leisure, while others regarded these things very firmly as work. Young and Willmott (1973) made the further point that many people do not see all their activities as simply either work or leisure. They allowed their respondents to categorise their activities as 'mixed' and these included travel to work, child care, shopping, personal care, eating, sleeping, adult education, civic and collective duties.

The Use of Leisure by Occupational Groups

How much leisure time people have and the ways in which they use it depend to a large extent on how much of their time and energies they invest in their occupations. Few studies have been made of the duration of leisure time for various occupational groups, no doubt partly because of the difficulty of defining leisure time. In the American suburban study by Lundberg and his associates (1934) in the early 1930s the average leisure time of male white-collar workers was reported as 438 minutes per day and that of executives as 401 minutes, but this included eating time. Without giving figures, Wilensky (1981) deduces from the comparative lengths of work weeks and work obligations that professionals, executives, officials and proprietors have less leisure time than the 'masses'. In Poland the daily estimated time spent as leisure was 3.5 hours for workers in manufacturing industries, 2 hours for railwaymen, 3 hours for clerks, teachers and engineers, and 2 hours for scientists and physicians (Strzeminska, 1966). It was noted that railwaymen read newspapers and even books during their working time, so their total time for leisure activities probably does not constitute an exception to Wilensky's broad generalisation.

Many more studies have been made of types of leisure behaviour by different occupational groups. The first national recreation survey in Britain (British Travel Association/University of Keele, 1967) showed that

the higher the income level, occupational class and educational status of contacts, the greater the number of pursuits they mentioned for their weekend before interview, and the greater the importance of the 'active' as compared with the 'passive' recreations. In short, those with the highest socio-economic status not only do more things, but do more active things. (p. 6)

Later government-sponsored and other surveys, in particular the General Household Survey reports for 1973, 1977 and 1980, confirm and expand these findings. Particularly striking are the differences in participation levels for outdoor sports (54 per cent for professional workers, falling to 14 per cent for unskilled workers). The only two activities more popular among manual workers were betting/doing the pools and playing bingo; the former was most popular with skilled manual workers, the latter with semi-skilled and unskilled workers.

Among employers and managers, 18 per cent play golf compared with less than 5 per cent in the manual groups. Soccer is predominantly the game of manual workers, while cricket is more popular among the non-manual. Income is not a factor in this last difference, because participation in the two games costs about the same. Soccer is on the whole a rougher and tougher game than cricket and may fit in better with a manual worker's idea of a manly sport. It is also a sport requiring closer co-operation between members of a team, reflecting more the content of working-class occupations than of individualistic middle-class occupations.

Veal (1982) has pointed out that the tendency, when discussing work–leisure relationships, to dichotomise occupations into middle-class/working-class or white-collar/blue-collar may be misleading. For example, taking five groups of activities (outdoor sport, indoor sport, watching live sport, informal outdoor recreation and informal indoor recreation) participation rates are *above* average for skilled manual workers and *below* average for junior non-manual workers. However, these are generalisations: skilled manual workers are selective in their pursuits, being more active in soccer, fishing, snooker, and so on, and less active in horse-riding, tennis and running. Similarly, junior non-manual workers, while being generally less active than skilled manual workers, do participate more than the average in riding, tennis, badminton and keep-fit. Veal rightly believes that analysis of leisure activities by a number of (as opposed to two) occupational groups may have a lot to tell us about the role of leisure in relation to the demands of work.

Various American studies confirm the conclusion that occupation is related to certain preferred ways of spending leisure. For example, Gerstl (1961) found that college professors spent less time with their children and around the home and less time on sport and non-professional organisations than did either advertising men or dentists. Graham (1959) concluded that the proportion of professional workers participating in strenuous exercise was nearly twice that of unskilled workers.

Other studies have been made in terms of wider class or status groups, which may reveal some occupational differences while obscuring others. According to White (1955), the upper middle class more often use libraries and have home diversions and lecture-study groups, while the two lowest classes more often use parks and playgrounds, 'community chest' organisations, churches, museums and community entertainment. Reissman (1954) found that those in higher class positions were more active and diverse in their social participation than those in lower classes and that the middle class tended to dominate the organisational activity of the community. Clarke (1956) concluded that 'spectatoritis' occurred most often at the middle level of occupational prestige and that craft interest tended to vary inversely with prestige level.

A study has been made of the leisure activities of a group of workers on rotating shifts, whose hours of work fall at all times of the day or night, during the week and at weekends (Blakelock, 1961). As compared with day workers, the rotating shift workers in this sample tended to belong to fewer organisations and to go to meetings less often, and had fewer activities in which participation can occur only at specific times. Activities, like visiting, that can occur at different times were less affected, and those that can occur at any time, like indoor work and hobbies, were increased.

Types of leisure may be classified in ways which straddle social and individual functions. One such typology is that of Noe (1970), who divides leisure into three forms – work, recreational and cultural. *Work* leisure incorporates any productive endeavour in which the role participant initiates the action, decides on the finished outcome and totally controls the means of production. This is an interesting integration of the concepts of work and leisure (a subject to which we shall return in later chapters) although Noe's formulation is unnecessarily individualistic and appears not to allow that decisions and controls may be in the hands of a group of co-operating individuals. *Recreational* leisure, according to Noe, includes any rule-rendering game activity in which the laws of chance, strategy, or skill govern the conduct of the players. *Cultural* leisure 'is any self-determined activity that maintains or reinforces the ideological heritage of a social system and provides for the creative pursuits of the self, manifested through the innovation of ideas and things'.

Noe's concept of work leisure is by no means the same as what Godbey (1975) calls anti-leisure: activity which is undertaken compulsively, as a means to an end, from a perception of necessity, with a high degree of externally imposed constraints, with considerable anxiety, with a high degree of time-consciousness and a minimum of personal autonomy. People who exhibit anti-leisure take their leisure as seriously as they take their work and 'work' just as hard at it

(Rothman and Mossman, 1972). Among the groups who find it hard to cope with unwanted free time are those who lose or are retired from jobs in which they were highly involved: they try to cope by building their 'leisure' on the model of their work.

The Meaning of Leisure

'The meaning of leisure in a given civilization depends on the meaning given to work ... What the individual demands of leisure depends on what he has and has not found in his work, and on what the education he has received has made him.' These propositions by Raymond Aron (1962) are consistent with such impressions and evidence as we have, but they can scarcely be said to have been adequately researched.

Most of the reported research on subjective meanings of leisure has been carried out by Havighurst and his associates. They did not use type of occupation as a specific variable, but some clues to the meaning of leisure for occupational groups can be gained from the analysis of social class groups. In a study of the leisure activities of a sample of middle-aged people in Kansas City, Havighurst (1957) concludes that different age, sex and social class groups can derive similar values from their leisure, even though its content is different. A comparative study was carried out in New Zealand, and leisure was found to have similar meanings in the two countries (Donald and Havighurst, 1959). In order of frequency, the principal meanings, defined as felt satisfactions or reasons for carrying on a particular leisure activity, were: (1) just for the pleasure of doing it; (2) a welcome change from work; (3) brings contact with friends; (4) gives new experience; (5) makes the time pass; and (6) gives the feeling of being creative. Certain differences according to sex and social class were found: for example, the 'creative' meaning was more often expressed by women and working-class people tended to stress the 'makes time pass' meaning (Havighurst, 1961).

Havighurst agrees with Aron that most of the meanings of leisure are also the meanings of work. In talking about their work, people say that they get all the satisfactions from work that they might get from leisure except that of a change from work. In comparing these meanings Havighurst states a general principle of the equivalence of work and play: to a considerable extent men and women can get the same satisfactions from leisure as from work. There are, of course, limitations to this principle. For instance, a person who has found friends at work and who values sociability with those friends may have very little further need for sociability during his leisure time. But when he retires he may find sociability in a non-work setting and thus substitute leisure for work satisfactorily, provided the other positive meanings that work had for him can also be continued by substitute activities. Happy retirement depends on the previous life a person has led and on his ability to preserve or transform the meanings that life has had for him.

In a further report Havighurst and Feigenbaum (1959) related leisure activity to social role performance. They distinguished two general patterns of lifestyle and leisure: community-centred and home-centred. They noted that these two patterns appeared to be equally accessible to middle-class people, but that working-class people were rarely community-centred. In about 5 per cent of cases lifestyle and leisure were not in close relation: these were people who invested most of their energy in work or in home and children, with little time or inclination for leisure. Another 6 per cent had a high level of leisure activity, but were dissatisfied or inadequate workers, parents, or spouses, who attempted to compensate with very active leisure time.

In this chapter I have considered the functions, activities and meanings involved in leisure. Three general conclusions emerge. First, the functions which leisure serves for society are rather different from those which apply to individuals: the former are to do with maintaining the social system and achieving collective aims, the latter provide relaxation, entertainment and personal development. Secondly, ways of spending leisure time tend to vary with the demands and satisfactions of the occupation, professionals and managers generally being more active than manual workers. And thirdly, the meanings found in leisure appear to be different for sex and social class groups, although the similarities hold between one industrial society and another.

5

Some Studies of Particular Groups

This chapter brings together the findings relevant to work and leisure of a series of studies which I have undertaken or participated in. Some of these studies covered topics other than work and leisure, but these are not dealt with here. Technical details about the samples (methods used to carry out the surveys, tests of statistical significance, and so on) are given elsewhere (see Parker, 1968).

Business and Service Workers

My first fieldwork, designed to include the study of work and leisure, consisted of 200 pilot interviews with people employed in 'business' and 'service' occupations. I wanted to start with occupations that were likely to have markedly different influences on the people working in them. My two groups were adapted from Blau and Scott's (1963) categories of business and service organisations, representing respectively organisations where the owners are the prime beneficiaries and those where the client group is the prime beneficiary. The two groups of occupations were known to differ in the content of the work and the way it was organised, and at this stage these were the main variables to be related to people's feelings about their jobs.

Psychologists maintain that people of certain personality types and with certain attitudes tend to seek out occupations that suit their personalities and attitudes. Research on the interests and values of people entering certain occupations or training courses confirms that this is generally the case (Duff and Cotgrove, 1982). Thus prospective businessmen tend to be interested in money and leisure, prospective social workers in the welfare of others, and so on (Simpson and Simpson, 1960). Without denying the importance of personality factors in the initial choice of an occupation, I wanted to concentrate on a rather different question: to what extent does the experience and meaning of work, and the work–leisure relationship, vary for people in different kinds of occupation? I also had in mind the possibility that occupations might shape the personalities and attitudes of those who stay in them for any length of time.

Asked what was the thing about their work that gave them most satisfaction, 69 per cent of the service workers mentioned something to do with their clients, compared with 24 per cent of business workers who mentioned something to do with their customers. Part of this difference was accounted for by the service people more often having client contact as a major part of their work than the business people had customer contact. But even when the 'non-contact' group was removed from the analysis, an occupational difference still remained. This indicates that while personal contact with those other than colleagues is a major source of satisfaction to people whose jobs entail this contact, more satisfaction is found in the service–client relationship than in the business–customer relationship.

Autonomy in the work situation was measured by the extent to which informants felt that they could determine the decisions or details connected with their jobs. The service people much more often reported having autonomy (76 per cent) than the business people (44 per cent). Much of the difference in autonomy between the two groups is explained by the different systems of management in the typical business concern and in the typical service organisation. A business organisation is more likely to be what Burns and Stalker (1961) call 'mechanistic', including specialisation of tasks, hierarchical control and frequent interaction between superior and subordinate. On the other hand, a service organisation is more likely to be 'organic', all its members doing the same sort of work, featuring control by small groups and frequent interaction between colleagues. The typical service job which consists of interviewing clients and helping to solve their personal problems can best be done with a maximum of individual discretion and a minimum of subjection to personal authority. But business efficiency is aided, at least up to a point, by bureaucracy and formal organisation and a consequent reduction of the area of individual discretion. Much of the autonomy found on the business side occurs where the work consists of dealing with people and much of the feeling of lack of autonomy on the service side arises from administrative demands. The latter situation is well illustrated by a young woman youth employment officer's remark: 'I have settled down to do things the way I want within the red tape.'

On the assumption that the degree to which a person feels 'used' or *extended* in his job is related to his other work experiences and attitudes, the question 'How much of your abilities and potentialities do you use in your work?' was asked. The business people more often said that they were limited by lack of scope in their job than the service people, but the difference was barely significant. There was a clearer trend to being limited by work pressures on the service side: ten out of twelve people who reported this kind of limitation were in service occupations. This often happened where case-loads were too heavy to allow much intensive case-work with individuals. As one young almoner put it: 'It's the days with perhaps four patients that bring out the most in you. With a quantity of patients you are worn out, but in a different way.'

A question on type of *involvement* in work allowed informants to choose 'self-expression', 'a way to earn', or both as descriptions of their own involvement. Among service informants, 67 per cent chose self-expression, compared with only 36 per cent among business informants. This difference is largely attributable to what is often called a vocational attitude to jobs in the service category. Although both types of occupation include those which provide services, the main object of the business concern is to make money, while the main object of the service organisation is to provide the service. It is not surprising, therefore, that employees in each type of occupation should reflect in their type of work involvement the main object of their employing body. A mosaic of the 'service' point of view shows how deep involvement can go:

> The job is a means of contributing socially; it consolidates my life and is part of settling down... In this type of work we are doing things on a broad scale – one feels it is a bit of social history in the making... I once got out of social work and missed it terribly. I felt guilty about having an easier job... This occupation is not just a means of earning or passing the time. It is difficult to visualise life without it... Work is now organising my life instead of I organising the work.

On the other hand the 'business' mosaic is less inner-directed and contains quite a strong feeling of being carried along with the majority:

> It's mainly a way of earning a living. Few people can see it otherwise... Most people, if they were honest, would say they work for money... As you get older with more family responsibilities it becomes more like earning a living... It's certainly not expressing yourself, writing little figures in books... You are caught and put in the cage so early you can't do much about it.

A further measure of occupational involvement is whether a person's present job is the one he would *choose* under other circumstances.

The question was put: 'If you could choose any occupation regardless of money which one would you choose?' Nearly three-quarters of the service people would still prefer their present occupation or something allied to it, compared with only 30 per cent of the business people. There was considerably more reluctance on the service side to consider changing jobs, or even to admit the existence of choice. 'I see life as living, as involvement rather than choosing this or that', as one young male youth employment officer put it. Sometimes the reason given for not desiring change was a practical one – 'this is the field in which I have most experience' – and sometimes a value judgement was made of the work itself. The remark of a female mental welfare officer, 'I couldn't do anything else – I wouldn't feel it was real work' – seems to be a view held by many whose work has a clear social purpose.

Several questions were put on aspects of the work–leisure relationship. With Dubin's (1956) concept of *central life interest* in mind, informants were asked 'What is your main interest in life?' and their answers were coded into broad categories. Among the business people only 11 per cent gave 'work' answers, compared with 29 per cent of service people; 78 per cent of business and 39 per cent of service people gave 'non-work' answers; and 11 per cent of business and 32 per cent of service people said they had no main interest.

Informants were asked whether they had as *close friends* any of the people they worked with. Of those in business occupations, 57 per cent said 'none', compared with only 22 per cent of those in service occupations. The explanation of this probably lies in the differences in objective work situations and in values attached to work. In many service occupations having friends in other jobs is in effect, if not in intention, discouraged. As one child care officer put it: 'This job makes outside contacts difficult to keep up because you can't rely on being able to keep evening appointments.'

Answers to the question 'Do you find that your work *encroaches* on your free time?' were classified as 'a lot', 'a little', or 'never'. Among the business informants, 68 per cent said 'never', compared with only 36 per cent among service informants. It was made clear in the interviews that the question was not concerned with irregular hours of work or overtime, but with voluntary activities connected with work, such as meetings and work-connected reading. The nature of the work seems to be an important factor in the extent of its spillover into free time. It is possible to let almost any job encroach on free time, but some types of work lend themselves to spillover and some do not. Thus a technical college lecturer said: 'I am always having to consider the next day's work or the next term's work, thinking about and preparing for classes.' But an insurance man, even with working hours often outside nine-to-five, was able to say: 'When I'm at home the iron curtain is dropped so far as work is concerned.'

Another phase of the analysis was to find out how far certain types of answer were correlated. It emerged that a cluster of variables was associated with the service occupations: having autonomy in the work situation, being fully extended in the job, having a self-expressive involvement in work, having central life interest in work, having work colleagues as close friends, and letting work encroach on leisure. The business occupations were associated with the negative of these variables – not having autonomy in the work situation, and so on.

An index of 'work involvement' composed of these items was applied to each of the ten occupational samples. Results suggested that, of the occupations studied, child care, mental welfare, teaching and being an almoner produce the greatest degree of work involvement as measured by the index, and banking, insurance, advertising and retail selling produce the least involvement. The occupations associated with high work involvement are all service occupations concerned with the problems and development of people; the occupations associated with low work involvement are in business and are concerned with impersonal things or with personal relations on a business basis.

The intermediate position of accountancy and youth employment is of special interest. Some of the accountants in the sample were working on their own account and retained some of the classic professional – client relationship, while the youth employment officers tended to feel themselves partly in the business world and partly in the social work world. Features of these two occupations draw attention to other occupations which are marginal between business and service: performing characteristically business work for a service organisation, and vice versa. A few supplementary interviews with people in such jobs (including an accountant working for a government body, and an interviewer in an employment agency) indicated that they had a 'split' attitude to their jobs, separating the service from the business element.

The results of these pilot interviews confirmed the initial hypothesis that people working in the business and service occupations differed markedly in their degree of work involvement. The results were also used to select three of the ten specific occupations for more intensive study and to provide a test of some of the questions to be used in that study.

Banking, Youth Employment, Child Care and Manual Workers

From the pilot interviews, child care officers were found to be one of the most work-involved groups and bank employees one of the least work-involved. Larger samples of these two groups, together with youth employment officers, who had an intermediate position on the scale, were sent questionnaires by post. A shorter version of the questionnaire was also sent to a mixed sample of manual workers, but for various reasons this must be regarded as a preliminary inquiry. Altogether, 425 people co-operated by returning usable forms.

The scope of the inquiry was the same as that of the pilot interviews, plus some questions on the amount and use of leisure time. The results of questions which were the same as, or similar to, those put in the pilot interviews generally confirmed that child care officers are typical of 'service' workers and bank employees of 'business' workers. The youth employment people gave answers generally more like those of child care officers than those of bank employees, thus confirming their kinship with the former as 'service' workers. The distribution of answers to other questions was as follows.

Information on *use of abilities* was gained from two questions, one on the number of abilities and the other on the extent to which they were used. Three in five of the youth employment and child care respondents, two in five of the manual workers, but only one in five of the bank employees felt that they used most of their abilities in their job. Very small proportions of youth employment and child care people felt that they used only a few of their abilities, but 28 per cent of bank employees and 25 per cent of manual workers felt this. Nearly three-quarters of bank respondents felt that they used their abilities in only a superficial or general way, compared with nearly half the youth employment sample and less than a third of the child care sample. Manual workers were not asked this question.

The measure of job *autonomy* used was different from that in the pilot interviews. Respondents were asked to say which of three methods of decision-making applied when changes had to be made or difficult problems solved in their jobs. In all three occupations the method most frequently reported was 'superior would decide after consultation with staff'. The second most frequent method given by youth employment and child care respondents was the more autonomous method 'decision taken at a meeting of all involved'. On the other hand, the less autonomous method 'superior would decide without consultation with staff' was given by a third of the bank people but by very few of the others. A few respondents in all occupations said that the decision was 'their own'.

Several questions were asked about the use of leisure. Concerning *membership of non-work organisations*, two-thirds of the youth employment and child care samples were active (holding office or being regular attenders) in at least one such organisation, compared with half the bank employees and a third of the manual workers. A breakdown of type of organisation membership showed that people in the three non-manual occupations were equally active in recreational organisations – about four in ten had at least one active membership – but among manual workers this proportion fell to one in ten. There was also a large occupational difference in membership of non-recreational organisations. This indicates that non-work obligations are more onerous for youth employment and child care employees than for those in banking and manual work.

Respondents were asked how many *hours of leisure* they normally had per week. It was clear that definitions of what constitutes leisure vary considerably. A few respondents who reported having 100–130 hours of leisure each week had obviously deducted working and work-related time from the total week of 168 hours. At the other end of the scale, six respondents said they had six hours of leisure or less each week. However, two-thirds of all respondents stated their weekly hours of leisure at a figure between 25 and 50. The average hours reported by youth employment and child care employees were 33–34 and by bank and manual workers 42–43. There were only very small differences in the leisure time reported by men and women and by the married and the single in the sample.

Something about *leisure preferences* was discovered by asking 'If you had an extra two hours each day, how would you prefer to spend them?' Some interesting occupational differences emerged. The bank people much less often preferred reading, and more often chose out-of-doors and sporting activities or to relax or sleep. The manual workers had the most home-centred choices, partly because they had the highest proportion of married respondents. The differences in the choice of work or study were small, but from comments made by youth employment and child care people about the type of reading which would be chosen it appears that this is often background reading to the job.

Respondents were asked about their *reasons for enjoying leisure*. They were given the alternatives: 'because it satisfies the interests that you *would like* to satisfy in your work', 'because it is satisfying in a *different way* from your work', or 'because it is *completely different* from your work'. Most respondents chose the second or third alternative, possibly because the idea behind the first is not clear. The bank people most often said 'completely different from work' and the youth employment and child care people 'satisfying in a different way'. The typical banking answer indicates a greater polarisation of leisure and work as satisfying and unsatisfying, while the other answer suggests that both leisure and work are found satisfying in their different ways.

Information on how respondents felt their *leisure differed from their work* was obtained from the choice among: 'completely different', 'a lot of free time taken up by things connected with work', or 'a little free time taken up by such things'. About three-quarters of the bank and manual workers said that their leisure was completely different from their work, as against a quarter of the youth employment people and a third of those in child care. Nearly a third of the youth employment and child care workers claimed that matters connected with work took up a lot of their free time, but only very small proportions of the bank and manual workers said this.

The groups using most or some of their abilities in their jobs were compared on two non-work questions with those using only a few of their abilities. The former were more likely to be active in, or members of, at least one non-work organisation (78 per cent) than were those who used only a few of their abilities (57 per cent). A higher proportion (25 per cent) of those using most or some of their abilities would prefer to spend extra free time reading or studying than would those using only a few of their abilities (9 per cent). These last two findings have special implications for the claim that those who fail to find self-expression and a sense of achievement in their work may turn to non-work life to find it. The present evidence is that those who find work more demanding of their abilities are more likely to be socially or intellectually active in their leisure than are those who find work less demanding. Non-involvement in work seems more likely to discourage than to facilitate involvement in leisure.

A question put only to manual workers concerned the *meaning* of leisure. Pilot inquiries showed that most people agreed with one of three types of definition, and these were put on the schedule. By arrangement, Dr Swift of Liverpool University also included this question in his interviews with paid social workers, and I quote from his unpublished results. The manual workers in the sample differed little from the social workers in their pattern of answers: 73 per cent of manual workers (77 per cent of social workers) thought leisure meant 'only the time you feel free to do whatever you like'; 16 per cent (14 per cent) thought it meant 'all the time you are not actually at work'; and 11 per cent (5 per cent) 'all the time except when working or doing essential things like eating and sleeping'. This suggests that most people tend to define leisure in a positive rather than a residual way, and it confirms the dimensions ('time' and 'feeling free') which our earlier definition embraced.

There was a tendency among manual workers, for those who thought their work was skilled and who used most of their abilities in their job, to define leisure more often as freedom compared with those who thought their work was less skilled and used fewer of their abilities. One possible explanation of this difference is that the residual definitions indicate a polarity of work and leisure. They are, therefore, more likely to be chosen by those who have a negative or neutral attitude to work. It may, however, be argued that the 'positive' response implies that freedom is obtainable only in leisure, and therefore that those who experience some degree of freedom in their work should be inclined to reject this definition. Perhaps those who are in skilled jobs using most of their abilities do feel less free, in the sense of being more committed to their work. More definite conclusions on these points must await further research.

To sum up, there seem to be two broad patterns of work and leisure experiences and attitudes among the groups sampled. On the one hand, people in banking and the less skilled kinds of manual jobs are comparatively uninvolved in their work, 'privatised' in their leisure and polar in their conceptions of leisure and work. On the other hand, the youth employment, child care and, to some extent, the skilled manual workers are involved in their work, are more socially and intellectually active in their leisure and have a more integrated conception of leisure and work. These are tentative and very broad conclusions and (especially in the case of manual workers) based on research that needs to be repeated and expanded. But they point to the pervasive influences of work on non-work experiences and cast doubt on the proposition that men and women can make up in their leisure for what they lack in their work.

Residential Social Workers

Almost by definition, social workers are more dedicated to their work than are people in most other occupations. But the small group of social workers who both live and work on the same premises are even more removed from the ordinary conditions of nine-to-five jobs than are non-residential social workers. For the former, work and leisure do not have the same meaning or the same separateness as they have for most other men and women. In an attempt to find out more about the way residential social workers pattern their lives, six case studies were carried out.

Case Study 1
Mr A, a middle-aged bachelor, is the director of a trust whose main function is to run a community for the homeless and destitute, a large proportion of whom are meths drinkers. In order to establish and maintain a proper human relationship with every person who comes for assistance, Mr A and his associates identify themselves to a large extent with those they are trying to help. They think of themselves, equally, as 'misfits' and refer to the 'square world' of the outside. Mr A is completely dedicated to his very demanding work. His activities

are of two main kinds: dealing with the men, including organising the community and sending out teams to bring into the community those in need of help; and the public relations effort of getting support for the work, including maintaining active contact with other social services to their mutual benefit.

Leisure in the accepted sense is non-existent in Mr A's life. His only diversion is a weekly visit to his ageing mother in the country. He has no urge to use part of his time away from his work situation to escape its demands or its stresses. Relaxation is necessary to him, but this does not imply withdrawal. 'I am relaxing now – I relax when I am with the men in the evening.'

Case Study 2

Mr B is a church social worker. Those who have personal problems may receive advice from him in the form of counselling or befriending. The unit is manned by a small non-residential staff; Mr B is the only member who has living quarters on the premises, and the only access to his living quarters is through the office. Each evening at eleven the phone is switched through to his apartment and he alone deals with night calls.

Mr B is unmarried and his friends are mostly social workers or men of the church. He rarely goes to parties or places of entertainment except when accompanying a friend or client, but he feels that he leads quite a full social life through his work. His occasional day off is not the conventional day away from the work situation. It simply consists in announcing to the office staff that he is having a day off, so that if he happens not to be available they can tell callers this. Otherwise it appears that his days off are very much the same as other days.

He can give no estimate of how much leisure he normally has, nor even of what to count as leisure. 'I am in my room of an evening and the vicar comes to call. We chat about various matters. He represents my employer but he is also my friend. I don't know whether to call this work or leisure.' He identifies 'free time' as time during which he is not committed to see anyone. Asked about his hobbies, he will give a characteristic answer: 'My hobbies are psychopaths and alcoholics.'

Case Study 3

Father C is an elderly Catholic priest. In addition to the usual duties of a priest, he has assumed many other civic duties. He lives in the presbytery attached to the church and is assisted by another priest.

Father C believes in being 'approachable and available' to those who need him. 'For my leisure I work, for my play I work, my hobby is work. The one thing that keeps me from cracking up is variety – different people, each with their different problems.' He is entitled to a regular day off each week but does not take this. If he has to visit a country or seaside town for a conference or meeting he will take a few hours off to relax while there. But he never takes such a trip for the purpose of leisure alone.

Does he have any free time? 'Yes – between appointments.' But the working day is so full that there is usually very little such free time. He has many close friends in all walks of life. He agrees that he has a good social life, but says this is mainly in the course of his work. He regards making speeches, which he is often called upon to do, not as a chore but as a convivial activity. It is probably this unserious attitude to many of his duties that enables him to live almost entirely within the realm of work.

Case Study 4

Mr D is the administrator-cum-warden of a residential hostel housing about forty men, some of whom come from prisons and mental hospitals. He has two assistants, plus four on the domestic staff. He has a wife and three small children and they live in a flat upstairs.

Mr D leads a remarkably busy life. There were periods in the past when he was without assistants, and as the two he has at present are young and fairly inexperienced, the men prefer to come to him with their problems. So the time that he is 'free', in a realistic sense, is rare. The residents are fairly understanding, but there is nearly always someone who needs attention. Whether or not he is 'off duty', he will make time to attend to these people and it is not uncommon for the residents to call upon him and his wife when they are in their own quarters.

'I am not really an organised man', says Mr D, though not as a point of pride. The house is like a large family home where people address each other by their Christian names. There is a remarkably relaxed atmosphere around Mr D, which belies the heavy burdens of his work. 'By nature I am a man of leisure', he says, 'and leisure is very important to me.'

Case Study 5

Miss E is matron of a small mother and baby home. She has an assistant and a small part-time staff. Her work is varied and includes keeping records as well as looking after the twenty or so mothers and their children. Officially she has one full and two half days off a week, but since the home is understaffed she often uses the half days to catch up on necessary paper work. She admits that she spends a lot of time talking with her friends about her work, but one or two of them are not at all interested in it and she thinks this is a good thing, as it gives her a wider horizon.

'You have to give your whole life to this sort of work', she says, with a touch of regret. When she was assistant matron she used to attend evening classes but, with increased responsibilities, she had to give those up. Today she has nothing she would call hobbies or spare-time interests. In addition to her own room upstairs, she has a sitting-room which she shares with her assistant and next door to this is a small office. She can relax in the sitting-room, but is quite often disturbed by the phone or by someone wanting to see her. Since her working day often consists of fourteen hours on duty, she takes whatever breaks she can between doing things and seeing people.

Case Study 6

Mr F is a young man who used to be in the business world and has only recently begun in the field of social work. He is employed in a rehabilitation centre with over thirty residents. He is reluctant to use the word 'vocational' about his work. He seems to regard it as incidental that his average working day is from twelve to sixteen hours, depending on whether or not it is his turn to wake the residents at 6.30 a.m.

His work sometimes comes all at once when various people or matters need attention, but there are other periods when little or nothing is going on. It is usually possible for him to have an hour or two off during the day.

Mr F feels an active concern for the residents, but maintains that he does not become emotionally involved in the process. 'Leisure in the proper sense means the time that I am away from the building; it is to be regarded as a matter of geography.' His off-duty days average eight per month. On these occasions he feels that he is able to extricate himself both physically and emotionally from his work ties. Apart from his enjoyment of music, his idea of leisure consists of meeting friends – none of whom is in social work – and going to the theatre and for long walks in the country.

Each one of these case studies is interesting for what it tells us about the lives of the people concerned, but collectively they are also of interest for what they can tell us about the similarities and differences of life patterns. Some writers prefer to rely entirely on case studies in describing life patterns. Thus Ronald Fraser (1968), in introducing the first volume of *Work – Twenty Personal Accounts*, criticises the sociological approach which he thinks 'tends to turn people into objects'. But he admits that 'the particular individual is always a part – indeed a product – of his society', and this points to the need for some kind of sociological analysis.

If the case studies are to amount to something more than anecdotes we need to ask what their sociological significance is. Residential social workers are an extreme example of a category of men and women who are disposed, by the type of work they do and the circumstances in which they do it, to show a pattern of work and leisure. The demands of the job vary among each of the six individuals studied, and so does their attitude to work and leisure. The case studies show how similar work situations in some ways induce a pattern of work and leisure shared by the group and in other ways allow differences in the ways in which people play their occupational and non-work roles. The group pattern included the following variables:

(1) *Relating to work situation*
Workplace and living quarters are co-extensive.
Work consists of helping people.
Work tends to expand to fill the total time in residence.

(2) *Relating to work and leisure*
There is willingness to work during official time off.
There are 'cases' of leisure in the working day.
'Free time' is equated with lack of responsibility for others.

The individual differences in attitudes to work and leisure apparent among the six people may be related to differences in their work situations. Mr A and Mr F represent two extremes and the following statements apply to Mr A, with those applying to Mr F in parentheses:

(1) *Work situation*
Workplace and living quarters are highly (partly) co-extensive.
Work consists of a variety (limited number) of ways of helping people.
Work expands to fill the total time in residence almost completely (partly).

(2) *Work and leisure*
Activities of work and leisure are very similar (dissimilar).
Social contacts are almost entirely (not) in the same type of work.
There is a high (low) level of emotional involvement in the work.
The caseworker role is conceived as extensive (limited).

The other four people fall somewhere between these two extremes. The interviews suggest that, with each of the six, the more dissimilar they are in their work situation, the more they tend to be dissimilar in their pattern of work and leisure. In short, we may conclude that residential social workers as a group differ in their work and leisure patterns from other workers, but also differ among themselves in the extent to which they are physically and psychologically committed to their work.

Local Government Councillors

We noted in Chapter 1 that the total space of non-work time is divisible for most people into 'pure' leisure (or freedom from obligations) and non-work obligations which they incur in meeting the necessities of life, in the service of their families or of other sections of the community. These non-work obligations may be placed on a scale of necessity–choice. Obligations to oneself by way of sleeping and eating have the minimum element of choice in them. Towards the middle of the scale are the obligations to one's family; these are conditioned by two types of choice – whether to assume responsibility for parents or other relatives and whether to marry or have children. At the end of the scale, where non-work obligations most closely resemble freely chosen leisure pursuits, come those activities which some men and women voluntarily perform in the service of groups outside their own families.

One of the many ways in which individuals may render public service is by being elected to their local council. No payment is given for the work, although councillors are entitled to claim for refund of expenses of various kinds. In many cases council and committee meetings take place in the evenings so that those in full-time employment may attend. Not only do councillors receive no pay for their public service, they also have to give up a considerable amount of their free time to perform it. Obviously they must gain some compensating satisfaction from this work.

A report made by the Government Social Survey (Moss and Parker, 1967) to the Maud Committee on People in Local Government includes data which throw light on the role of council service in the lives of those who take part as elected representatives. In addition to factual information from a sample of over 3,000 councillors and aldermen in England and Wales, interviews with a sub-sample of 598 were obtained and questions put on various aspects of council service and opinions on it. Although no questions were asked about councillors' leisure habits, the information they gave about the role of council work in their lives tells us something about the experience of 'work in leisure'.

An occupational difference was found in the amount of time spent on council work. Manual workers spent about 30 per cent more than the average of 52 hours a month, while small employers, managers and farmers (as a group) spent about 20 per cent less. Some of this difference is accounted for by the clustering of occupational groups in certain types of council: the fact that farmers are heavily over-represented on rural district councils, on which relatively little time is spent, helps to explain why the group that included farmers put in less time. But, even allowing for this, an occupational difference in time spent on council work still remains.

The survey provided data on why people take up council work and the gains and losses involved. Informants were asked whether being a councillor had affected their private life. Younger councillors (under 45) more often said that their private lives had suffered and less often that they had been helped, and these proportions were reversed among older councillors (65 and over). However, an adverse effect on private life does not necessarily follow from time spent on council work: the younger councillors just spent rather less time on it than did the older ones. Greater family responsibilities among younger councillors and the greater time available to the older and retired ones probably account for this.

The various socioeconomic groups were fairly evenly divided between those reporting adverse and favourable effects on private life, except that nearly twice as many manual workers as the average said that it had suffered. It seems that the families of manual-worker councillors are less likely than the families of other types of councillor to accept without protest the inroads which council work makes into free time. Also, the fact that being a councillor less often helps the private lives of manual workers may be partly explained by council experience having less relevance to their daily lives than it has for other types of councillor.

Informants were asked whether being a councillor had given them the opportunity of using abilities which they otherwise would not have used. The proportion who agreed that council work had given them such opportunities varied from 52 per cent of large employers, managers and professionals to 82 per cent of manual workers. There was also some difference in the ways in which potential abilities were felt to be used. The non-manual and manual worker groups were more likely than others to say that they had had opportunities for public speaking, widening their outlook and knowledge, and using organising and administrative abilities. These are obviously the kind of abilities which few of them would have been able to exercise in the course of their daily occupations.

A more detailed breakdown of the answers by particular socioeconomic groups showed even wider differences. Thus 100 per cent of the small group of foremen and supervisors said that council work had given them the opportunity of using potential abilities, compared with only 33 per cent among the self-employed professional workers. Clearly, the latter often have a working life which uses most of their abilities, whereas manual-worker councillors, whose abilities have presumably led to their becoming foremen or supervisors, may feel that their potential is even better used in council work.

The influence of council work in developing potential abilities is illustrated by what councillors said in answer to the question about it. The following is a selection of typical comments:

It has brought out a lot in me – you surprise yourself that you're able to grasp so many details and so much knowledge of a wide variety of things.
If I didn't do this I would just be in a dead end job. It has sharpened my outlook and attitude – I understand people's problems better.
I am not an educated man, but over the years I have been able to build up great confidence in myself. Thirty years ago I would never have dreamt of public speaking.

Just under a third of the employed councillors interviewed found council work more satisfying than their daily occupation, a third preferred their occupation and just over a third said they enjoyed both. More than half of the older councillors enjoyed both council work and occupation; council work was more often satisfying among the middle-aged councillors and occupation was most satisfying among the younger ones. Younger councillors tend more often than older ones to be in professional and intermediate non-manual occupations such as teaching and welfare work. Some of these young councillors are at a stage in their occupational careers when they are just beginning to establish themselves and perhaps also have the responsibilities of early married life. In these circumstances it would not be surprising if council work were to be seen as a kind of supplement to other aspects of life in general and to occupational life in particular.

Among middle-aged councillors council work often becomes more satisfying than occupation. During this period of life, it may be that some individuals find that they have got as far as they can in their daily occupation and turn to outside interests – for example, council work – for satisfaction and a fresh sense of achievement. If men and women do not find their occupation demanding or rewarding enough, they may well undertake council work for a sense of self-realisation. Council work, then, may sometimes be a form of compensation for some kind of shortcoming felt in occupational life.

Councillors aged 65 and over appear to find occupation (when they still have one) and council work equally rewarding. At this age continuation in an occupation is likely to be voluntary. But 20 per cent of all councillors are retired and for these, more than for employed councillors, public service must often become an important source of fulfilment and identity. For the retired we may say that council work is likely to be a substitute for a paid occupation. It is relevant to note that among aldermen (48 per cent of whom are 65 or over) occupation is found more satisfying than council work by only 12 per cent.

So far it has been suggested that there are three types of relationship of council work to occupation: as supplement, as compensation and as substitute. A consideration of the attitudes of councillors in the various socioeconomic groups helps to test this hypothesis. Only 13 per cent of employers, managers, professionals and farmers found council work more satisfying than occupation, compared with 64 per cent of manual workers. It seems that whatever satisfactions most of the former group get from council work they are also able to get from their occupations. This would be consistent with their regarding council work as a supplement to occupation, at least in terms of providing personal satisfactions. For councillors whose jobs are more routine and offer less scope, however, council work is clearly often a means of obtaining satisfactions not offered by their occupations – their council work functions as compensation for the limitations of their daily jobs.

A more detailed breakdown of particular socioeconomic groups shows even wider differences. Only one self-employed professional councillor (representing 3 per cent of his group) claimed to enjoy council work more than occupation, compared with 74 per cent among the semi-skilled manual-worker councillors. Also, the foremen and supervisors in the manual–worker group were closer to the non-manual and employer groups in their lesser preference for council work. It seems that the job of foreman or supervisor is likely to offer personal satisfactions closer to those of council work and it is the ordinary manual-worker councillors who tend to find their major satisfactions outside their jobs and through council work.

Informants were asked whether being a councillor had affected their relations with people involved in their daily occupation. The employers, managers, professionals and farmers less often had work relations affected than had the non-manual and manual workers. The last two groups more often had work relations affected both for the better and for the worse. The most frequent ways in which work relations were affected for the better were that informants felt they were more respected by colleagues and that their circle was extended. Typical comments were:

I have rather more prestige – the managers of my firm respect me, too.

Becoming a councillor affected recognition in my company – I was promoted soon afterwards.

The most frequent ways in which work relations were affected for the worse were that business was lost, people were offended, or work relations were made more difficult. Thus:

You need a lot of time off – this affects one's colleagues and they tend to view you as a bit of a nuisance – especially your immediate superiors.

I have to meet 250 people per week – they often ask me to help and when I can't I lose business because they don't buy through me any more.

A measure of general satisfaction with council work is the frequency of giving it up or wanting to give it up. The rank order of turnover of socioeconomic groups on councils is the same as the rank order of proportions intending to give it up after a while or in the near future – the large employers, managers and professionals highest and the manual workers lowest. Professional and self-employed councillors have a turnover rate more than 50 per cent above the average. Only 1 per cent of manual workers intended to give up council work soon, compared with 12–14 per cent in the other socioeconomic groups.

It seems reasonable to conclude that council work fulfils characteristically different functions in the lives of men and women in the various occupational groups. The fact that proportionately more employers, managers and professionals are councillors than are those in other occupations indicates that the former kinds of employment, and the experience gained in them, are similar to those of council work. The method of recruitment is obviously a factor in determining the kind of people who join councils, but the political parties and other sponsoring agencies can only bring in those who can be persuaded to stand. Relatively few manual workers have so far been persuaded to stand or have put themselves forward for election, and the present manual-worker councillors are probably very unrepresentative in many ways of manual workers generally.

It is remarkable that those manual workers who are brought into council work appear to get much more involved in it than do other types of councillor – they spend more time on it, their private lives more often suffer because of it, they more often use potential abilities in it and they less often want to give it up. For many of them, council service seems to have the strong motive of compensation for short-comings felt in occupational life. To a lesser extent, this also seems to be true of the non-manual workers' group. The relation between occupation and council work for this type of councillor may be called one of opposition. The content of, and types of, social relationship involved in his daily occupation and his council work are usually very different. He more often has difficulty with both his family and his work relations because council work is in a sense an alien experience – and probably it is often not 'expected of him'.

Rather different factors enter into the motivation of employers, managers and professionals to become councillors. The kind of work they do for a living – dealing with people, studying documents, making administrative or policy decisions – has much in common with their work as councillors. Their occupational obligations may well intrude into time which could be given to council work, and not surprisingly they spend less than the average time on it. In the case of self-employed professionals, not only do they fail to feel a sense of using potential abilities in council work, they also have a greater tendency to give it up. This all adds up to a weaker motivation to serve on councils – one of supplementing a fairly full and self-express-ive working life. They may share with manual-worker councillors the motive of public service, but they do not have such a personal need for council work and the satisfactions it can bring. In terms of work and leisure, council work is an extension of their occupational life. This extension pattern would also apply to many retired councillors, in that council work is to some extent a substitute for the interest and involvement that they had in their occupations.

Differences between the extension and opposition patterns lie partly in occupational experience and partly in council experience. If those whose occupations involve administrative work or making policy decisions find their major satisfaction (or at least sense of social useful-ness) in this aspect of council work then there is some continuity between the two roles. On the other hand, much council work con-sists of dealing with the problems of individuals, and neither this nor policy-making may have much in common with the occupational experiences of most manual-worker councillors.

Being a rural district councillor is not such an onerous business as being a county borough councillor. Farmer employers and managers account for 30 per cent of rural district councillors, and these may be seen as a third group in terms of the relation between occupation and council work. They put in less time as councillors and more often prefer their occupation to council work, but they do feel they use potential abilities as councillors and they do tend to remain longer than other types. They experience less of the competition between occupation and council work that many of those with the extension pattern do. Instead, they seem to have worked out a middling pattern of neutrality between occupation and council work, which may help to explain why proportionately so many farmer employers or managers are councillors.

Most of the above analysis has been concerned with the relation between council work and occupation. Council work is one kind of non-work obligation, and whether such obligations are undertaken depends to some extent on the willingness to forgo leisure pursuits. Unfortunately no questions were asked in the survey about councillors' leisure, so it is not possible to present any evidence concerning the possible interrelationship between occupation, council work and leisure. We do, however, know that councillors spend on average about twelve hours a week on their public duties and some spend substantially more than this. For them, as for the residential social workers discussed in the previous section, leisure of the conventional type must be very scarce and sometimes even non-existent. It seems likely that councillors are generally recruited from that section of the population whose leisure needs are low. Perhaps it is not uncharitable to suggest that councillors are sometimes able to find leisure-like experiences and satisfactions in the course of performing their public duties.

6

The Unwaged: Housewives, the Unemployed and the Retired

The groups whose patterns of life I considered in the previous chapter – business and social workers and local government councillors – were selected because the nature of their out-of-home work could be shown to have a marked influence on their leisure (and, to a lesser extent, vice versa). The groups to be considered in this chapter (who may be collectively described as the unwaged and who constitute nearly half the adult population) do not have out-of-home paid work, although most of their members have experienced such work in the past and some may experience it in the future. Writers on work and leisure (including myself) have been accused of concentrating too much on full-time workers (mostly men) and too little on other groups (including many women) who do not have full-time work (McIntosh, 1981). Indeed, the scheme for analysing life space presented in Chapter 1 is explicitly based on the constraints and opportunities experienced by full-time workers. In this chapter, therefore, I aim to discuss the work and leisure lives of groups without waged work.

Housewives

I am intentionally going to deal here principally with the category 'housewives' rather than 'women'. Unmarried women (except most of those over pension age) normally have out-of-home jobs and although the patterns of both their jobs and their leisure behaviour do differ in some ways from those of men, the nature of their work–leisure relationships is not markedly affected by their gender. Married women who have full- or part-time jobs may have husbands who share in varying degrees the household and child-rearing tasks: if the husband's share is minimal, then their work and leisure lives may approximate to those of unmarried working women. But it is the married women with no outside job – and especially those with young children to look after – who constitute the polar opposite case to the full-time employed. This is not, however, an exclusively female category: the small but growing number of 'househusbands' are in the same position of having work but no employment.

In Chapter 1 I outlined a scheme for analysing life space and pointed out that it applied mainly to the majority of men and substantial number of women who had out-of-home paid work. A number of amendments and qualifications to this scheme are necessary if it is to reflect the circumstances and attitudes of the general run of housewives today.

First of all, work: although they have no employment, housewives do have work – the work connected with running the home and looking after the children (husbands may, of course, share in this work, but we are discussing here the polar opposite case to that of men and women for whom 'work' consists mainly of employment). I have been taken to task for supposing that 'work', as used in my original analysis of life space, means that which is done for money, outside the home and as a distinct area of life, and it is claimed that these suppositions do not fit the case of housewives.

My answer is to accept the first of these suppositions but to question the second and third. While all employment has the characteristic of being undertaken for money, it is not necessarily done outside the home or as a distinct area of life. As we saw with residential social workers (both men and women) place of employment and home can be one and the same, so with housewives place of work and home are one and the same. The difference is that whereas residential social workers normally have part of the residence which is their own retreat where they can enjoy a certain amount of privacy and 'leisure', housewives are often less able to divide up their home in this way. (Better-off housewives, however, may live in homes which do enable them to have a room or two which is more or less their own territory.) Also, whether work is seen as a distinct area of life is partly a matter of work situation and partly of work and leisure attitudes. Housewives are not the only group for whom work is often not a distinct area of life – certain professional, craft and self-employed workers tend to have the same lack of demarcation between what is work and what is not.

My second category of life space (work obligations) is said not to apply to housewives. Certainly the example of voluntary overtime makes sense only for employed people, but the further example of having a second job may not be so inapplicable to housewives. Indeed, it may be a sensible way of conceptualising the part-time jobs which many housewives have – jobs, whether they consist of homeworking or the more usual outside employment, which do not provide the family's main source of income but which are necessary to supplement it.

Thirdly, there is existence time, or time for the satisfaction of physiological needs. I have suggested that these include sleep, eating, washing and eliminating, while recognising that sometimes, as with eating for pleasure, they can overlap with leisure. McIntosh (1981) sees 'an immediate problem here for a (married) woman . . . she is not simply doing these things for herself, but facilitating them in other people: feeding her husband, washing her invalid mother-in-law, changing the baby's nappies'. McIntosh apparently attributes to me a distinction between ensuring one's own existence and facilitating that of others. But I see no reason why the category of 'existence time' cannot be used in both these senses, so that it applies to housewives as well as others, albeit with more emphasis among housewives on meeting the physiological needs of others as well as their own.

Fourthly, we have non-work obligations, or semi-leisure. McIntosh is quite right to point out that, while this can be a fairly peripheral category of time for most men (and for many fully employed women), for the housewife it 'fills a large part of her day'. After allowing for the satisfaction of physiological needs it is 'the sum total of her work in the home'.

Lastly, we come to leisure, which I have defined (admittedly somewhat residually) as 'time free from obligations to self or to others – time in which to do as one chooses'. There is no suggestion that this is a gender-biased category; rather it is claimed that housewives have very little of this time, that facilities are inadequate for their leisure and that their freedom to enjoy it is often constrained by men.

Time budget studies show that women with paid jobs, whether full or part time, have less free time than men; housewives have more free time than men, but only on weekdays (Szalai, 1972). However, the total amount of free time tells us nothing about its distribution during the working day and weekend. As Talbot (1979) points out, unexpected periods or scattered amounts of free time may be less easy to plan for than a more usable block of free time. Housewives are more likely than men to have irregular or unpredictable periods of free time which make commitment to formal activities or organisations difficult.

Time apart, it is the quality of leisure experience possible for housewives that has been the subject of widespread concern (Anderson, 1975; Coles, 1980; Deem, 1982). Because work and leisure are fused for the housewife with young children, she lacks a separate life space for work in terms of both time and location. As a corollary, the work of the housewife does not entail a separate supportive social network such as is often found at workplaces. Because of the obligations of housewifery, there are real constraints on opportunities for free choice both of leisure and of waged work activities. Moreover, there is a general belief among both women and men that married women do not need (or even have the right) to follow their own interests or develop any kind of social life outside their family. Unlike her wage-earning sister, the housewife is not readily able to extend her social contacts, particularly if she does not have the use of a car. It has also been suggested that because domestic labour is often not regarded as 'work', housewives are led to feel guilty about taking time off to pursue their own interests.

While accepting that the leisure of housewives tends to be constrained more than that of most men and employed women, it is reasonable to put another view concerning the meaning of their lives and their sources of enjoyment. Gregory (1982) questions how far we should be concerned with the 'lack of leisure space' available to non-employed mothers of young children. For such mothers the tasks of housewifery and of bringing up children are often undertaken in the context of commitment to the development of growing relationships within the whole family. Such a commitment colours attitudes to the work–leisure relationship, giving most activities qualities of both. For a housewife, the physical environment of the home area and the social cohesion of the local community are crucial to the achievement of a satisfying and integrated life. The fact that many systems and organisations still exploit women does not negate the achievements of some housewives in developing values and cultures different from those of full-time employees and which benefit themselves and society.

The Unemployed

In all advanced industrial and capitalist countries unemployment has been increasing in recent years and the trend is still upwards. Different countries, different industries and different occupations have been variously affected, and it has been pointed out (Roberts, 1981) that, rather than there having been a net loss of jobs, the labour force has grown more quickly than the demand for labour. Whatever the explanation of unemployment, however, it clearly affects many millions of people and presents problems both to the individuals and families concerned and to the socieities which have to bear the cost of lost production and services.

Since the unemployed have no work – or, more precisely, no employment – it may reasonably be supposed that they have more time for leisure than the average worker. But leisure is more than just a space of time: it implies relative freedom from constraint. Unfortunately, the unemployed are constrained in several ways: financially, socially, morally and in terms of the structure of their daily lives (Smith and Simpkins, 1980; Corrigan, 1982). Unemployment benefit, the main source of income for those without paid jobs, has traditionally been, and remains today, much below average earnings of the employed. The income of many unemployed men and women, far from affording a reasonable material standard of leisure living, is below what may be considered a minimum level of support needed for even a very simple lifestyle and frugal existence.

Socially, the unemployed are constrained in various ways affecting relationships with family and friends. Although some married couples welcome the extra time they can spend together because of unemployment of the husband or both spouses, others find that it leads to domestic conflict in the home. Feelings of economic and social inadequacy increase, and the domestic situation may become generally tense. Leisure pursuits and social life outside the home are curtailed: visits to the pub and other places of entertainment have to be cut down or given up entirely. Those who had cars when they were in work may have to give them up, so that visits to relatives and friends become rarer (Hill, 1978).

There is considerable evidence that the 'leisure' of the unemployed is not experienced as leisure at all. Some of the reasons for this are:

(1) *Leisure is still commonly thought of as only possible in relation to employment.* The high positive value placed on work in our society means that a negative value is placed on unemployment. As Smith and Simpkins (1980) point out, social worth and the work ethic are powerfully related. The experience of unemployment and the status of being unemployed lead to an internalised moral condemnation which reflects the prevailing although hopefully weakening view that anyone who is not employed is not really a 'fully paid up' member of society. In these circumstances, the unemployed are effectively denied access to those forms and meanings of leisure which are deemed to be the reward for work.

(2) *For the unemployed, the sense of time tends to disintegrate.* Studies in the 1930s and more recently show that being unemployed is something very different from having leisure time (Jahoda, 1979). The unemployed frequently experience disintegration of their sense of time. Having nothing to do means that they become less able to be punctual for meals or other social commitments. The loss of a settled framework provided by the job and its daily routine, combined with a decreased awareness of the passage of time and a kind of apathetic attitude towards it, unite to make family life – the normal context for many leisure activities – more difficult for the unemployed man or woman. This particularly applies to men, for whom the alienating effects of being workless are more severe than for women, who more often have a separate source of identity and social worth in terms of family and motherhood.

(3) *The unemployed are subject to stress in personal and social life.* The
New Depression, as Forester (1976) describes it, has brought an
increase in suicide, attempted suicide and calls to organisations
such as the Samaritans. Youth unemployment, in particular, is
taking its toll on mental health and may literally be driving some
young people to suicide. Although the content and conditions of
much employment are not especially satisfying, the shared
experience with others outside the family is valued, and unemployment brings the demoralising effect of social isolation.
Within the family, relationships are strained, even if both spouses
overtly face the crisis and deprivation in a spirit of togetherness.

(4) *Unemployment is characterised as a deviant status.* The deviant status
of the unemployed is manifested in a number of different ways.
Their behaviour differs from that of employed people: they stay
at home when others are at work, are priced out of many leisure
activities, and so on. They often come to accept that they are
deviant – later if not at first. Their categorisation is formally
confirmed, since they have to report weekly or fortnightly to
receive their unemployment benefit. In these and other ways the
deviant status of the unemployed is established and reinforced,
helping to make it difficult for them to participate in leisure
activities on equal terms with the majority of employed men and
women.

Studies of the human consequences of unemployment suggest
that there are sequential phases of reaction and adjustment. Hill
(1978) categorises these as initial responses, the intermediate
phase and settling down to unemployment. The initial response
to the loss of one's job can be traumatic, especially if it comes at
the end of a long period of steady employment. More often,
however, the response is one of denial and a feeling that nothing
much has happened. The individual regards himself as tempo-
rarily out of work, thinks that he will soon find another job and
maintains a certain feeling of optimism. He may even enjoy the
initial experience of unemployment, looking upon it as a holiday
or an opportunity to get overdue jobs done about the house.
Some literally take a holiday away from home, which helps
convince them that their situation is temporary.

These initial responses usually do not last for long and give
way to a second phase. Savings are exhausted, the holiday is
over, jobs around the home have been finished and the first few
applications for jobs have failed. The individual begins to accept
the identity and standard of living of an unemployed person.
Leisure takes on a different quality. One stays longer in bed,
watches more television, or just lazes about. It is one thing to

come home after a day's work and flop down in front of the
television, but quite another to watch it during the day simply
because you have nothing else to do. The unemployed develop a
kind of inertia that is psychologically debilitating. They feel
increasingly that they are becoming not only occupationally but
also psychologically de-skilled, less able either to search for work
or to overcome boredom and depression in their 'leisure'.

After a time the person begins to settle down to being unemployed. Anxiety, struggle and hope all decline, and the individual and his family adjust to the standard and lifestyle of the
long-term unemployed. The depression associated with the
intermediate phase may even lift. Habits stabilise and active
search for work ceases or takes place at a lower level. The
individual develops a domestic routine consistent with chronic
unemployment and adjusts to a leisure life severely restricted by
shortage of money.

There is every reason to agree with the view of Smith and Simpkins
(1980) that 'research on the unemployed leads to the finding that, in
terms of life style and the use of free time, the experience of unemployment is not leisure'. Although one of the main effects of being
unemployed is a substantial increase in the amount of free time at the
individual's disposal, this can hardly be construed as leisure or even as
liberation from work. Unemployment is for most of its victims an
economic disaster, and for those who are imbued with the work ethic
it can also lead to an internalised moral condemnation. For those who
can find an adequate alternative source of income to employment – via
the informal economy, ranging from neighbourhood organisations to
'black market' work – the effects are less severe and a more or less
normal leisure life may be possible. But these are the relatively few
people who have been able to transform an essentially negative condition of unemployment into a more positive way of life which is not
based on some form of employment.

The Retired

In everyday parlance the state of retirement is frequently associated
with the state of being at leisure. If leisure is defined residually as the
absence of work then the temptation to make the association is
increased, for retirement is also the absence of work. The credibility of
the association is further increased by thinking of both retirement and
leisure in terms of time rather than quality of activity or experience:
leisure is something for which we have time at the end of the working
day, week, year – and of the working life. Moreover, there is in the

conventional wisdom about work, retirement and leisure a means/end or effort/reward connection: after a lifetime of work, a person is thought to be entitled to a few years of well-earned leisure.

If work is an unpleasant means of earning a living, then the leisure of retirement is compensation for effort expended and time wasted. But if work is a positive experience then the leisure of retirement is not compensation but a replacement for something valued which has been lost. Whether work is experienced as positive or negative, pleasant or unpleasant, as an end in itself or only as a means to an end, anticipated leisure is at the core of the myth of retirement. It is appropriate to regard it as a myth because it is not the reality which many people experience in retirement. There is often an unrealistic expectation that the role of leisure will increase in retirement and an unjustified belief that leisure can offer adequate compensation or reward for the loss of work.

The notion that retirement can compensate for or replace work involves the belief that the role of leisure in the life of the individual will increase or change with the advent of retirement. The role of leisure in retirement has been the subject of a number of studies in recent years. In general, the findings emphasise continuity of lifestyle from the pre-retirement to the retirement period. Thus Atchley (1971) writes about a lifestyle developed in middle age which is retained as much as possible into old age, not so much in terms of simply maintaining activity levels but in terms of preserving a continuity of psychological commitment to a particular lifestyle.

Research evidence suggests that the ageing process does not normally bring about a fundamental change in the type or quality of leisure behaviour. There are differences between the ways in which retired and non-retired persons experience leisure, but there is no reason to suppose that 'retirement' leisure represents a dramatically new set of behaviours in more than a minority of cases. As Peppers (1976) puts it:

> contrary to the popular notion that retirement brings with it a prescribed group of 'acceptable' leisure pursuits, the subjects involved in this research were engaged in a wide range of activities, from gambling to reading, horse-breeding to bird-watching, golf to team sports. Perhaps the only general statement that can be made concerning the nature of leisure activity in retirement is that there is no specific retirement activity. (p. 445)

There is a persistent but ill-founded belief that the coming of retirement can bring a new dawn to the life pattern of the ageing individual. Optimistic statements about the enhanced role of leisure in retirement abound in the literature. For example, Friedmann (1958) refers to the years of retirement as the 'years in which man can live without the iron necessity of work. These are the years of leisure'. Hochschild (1973) makes the rather dramatic assertion that 'the old are the forerunners of a future leisured society' but at least he acknowledges that 'this position wins them no status in today's society, which clearly values work most highly'.

Many such statements linking retirement with the positive experience of leisure are derived from research on the circumstances and attitudes of the relatively prosperous retired in the middle-class USA. The picture does not hold for the elderly in many other industrial countries and among the poorer classes in the USA. What might be called the pessimistic view of retired persons' experience of leisure is well put by Simone de Beauvoir (1972):

> Leisure does not open up new possibilities for the retired man; just when he is at last set free from compulsion and restraint, the means of making use of his liberty are taken from him. He is condemned to stagnate in boredom and loneliness, a mere throw-out. (p. 6)

This view of retirement as a frustrating disappointment to those who looked forward to it is echoed by Samson (1972): 'There are so many people pathetically bored after a short while in retirement, so hopelessly at a loss to find contentment in the leisure for which they have worked so long, anticipated so eagerly.'

What are we to make of these widely differing assessments of the experience of leisure in retirement? No doubt there are extremes: some individuals make the transition from working life to retirement in an easy, well-prepared and entirely happy manner, while others suffer greatly from the change, are ill prepared for it and bitterly regret that it has to happen to them. But it seems reasonable to suppose that the majority of men and women fall somewhere between these two extremes. The interesting question for research is what the factors are which cause people to be at different points between the extremes and the important question for policy is how to make it possible for more people to be closer to the desirable extreme than to the undesirable.

The ways in which men and women approaching retirement view the role of leisure in the rest of their lives depend on a combination of prevailing social attitudes to leisure and the pattern of life which they have worked out for themselves. If the social attitudes to leisure are in a state of flux (as indeed they are in modern industrial societies) then what is selected by the individual from the range of possible attitudes may well be ones imbibed from childhood rather than those having gained more recent currency. People who have already retired will mostly have been brought up in a social atmosphere in which the values and judgements of the Protestant work ethic prevailed. Consequently, they will tend largely to measure self-worth and the degree of respect to be accorded to others in terms of doing paid work which gives them a social identity. Furthermore, they will usually view leisure as the reward for work and as conditional upon work, so that leisure without work may well induce conscious or unconscious feelings of guilt. Future generations of retired people are likely to have become more accustomed to leisure in its own right rather than as a reward for work, so they will probably have less difficulty in adjusting to leisure in retirement.

Retirement comes fairly easily to those who have developed a satisfying leisure life alongside their work activities, although the character and meaning of leisure may change if its relationship with work is lost. Even for those with plenty of hobbies or interests, the change is usually more than just a quantitative expansion of time for leisure. Part of the satisfaction of leisure consists in contrasting it with work which, although it may not be consciously satisfying, is bound up with deep feelings of identity and meaning. When an individual retires he must come to see that what he formerly considered peripheral activities are not only satisfying but also significant. These leisure activities have, in short, to substitute for the meaning attached to work.

To have leisure as part of an alternating pattern of work and non-work is one thing – to have 'leisure' all the time is likely to be quite another. The leisure activities of an employed person are usually accompanied by the knowledge that he will soon have to terminate them and return to his occupational commitments. By contrast, the expectations and interpretations of leisure for the retired person are non-structured and vague. He is in the position of having practically unlimited free time. But because leisure usually means something more than just free time, it would be a mistake to assume that because a retired person has a life of all (or nearly all) free time he therefore has a life of all (or nearly all) leisure.

7

The Work–Leisure Relationship

There is no strict dividing line between the separate studies of work and leisure and of the work–leisure relationship. In Chapters 3 and 4 I considered work and leisure separately, and in Chapters 5 and 6 I examined the life patterns of particular waged and unwaged groups. In this chapter I shall review research which concentrates on the relationship between work and leisure. The work and leisure patterns characteristic of certain occupational groups are first considered, followed by a detailed assessment of empirical studies of different types of work–leisure relationship. Next, work and leisure as alternative sources of central life interest are discussed and the chapter concludes with a weighing up of the pros and cons in the 'fusion versus polarity' debate.

Group Patterns

The studies discussed in earlier chapters were fairly straightforward accounts of the ways in which men and women in certain occupations or class groups typically spend their leisure time. A functional relationship may be inferred from some of the patterns of leisure (for example, a greater need for non-work physical exercise by white-collar workers) but we may turn to a further group of studies for a more explicit treatment of the work–leisure relationship.

Data are available on the relation between work and leisure typical of a wide variety of occupational groups. To consider first the manual group: the decreased physical strain of work has brought about a change in the function of leisure for some manual workers. Thus it has been observed that the jobs of steelworkers have now become so relatively lacking in strain that the worker leaves the plant with a good deal of energy left which carries him readily through his leisure hours. However, in mining, fishing and some manual occupations leisure tends to have a more traditional role. Tunstall's (1962) study of distant-water fishermen showed that leisure during the three months in the year they are ashore fulfils the functions of status-seeking and of explosive compensation for physically damaging work. Some of the favoured leisure activities of pipelayers in the construction industry – fighting, drug-taking, stealing and promiscuous sex – also show marked evidence of compensation for tough working conditions (Tucker, 1981).

Something of this violent reaction to work can be seen in the leisure activities of some non-manual workers. Friedmann (1960) quotes a study of the leisure habits of employees at the Postal Cheque Centre in Paris, whose jobs are completely routine: on leaving the office, these clerks are either much more active or, in contrast, withdraw into themselves in a sort of apathy. Staff in the management services department of a large British corporation also showed a predominant pattern of home-centred leisure, consisting mainly of working around the home, engaging in hobbies and do-it-yourself activities, watching television and reading (Lansbury, 1974). But a more integrated pattern of work and leisure is shown by those non-manual employees whose work demands more involvement and responsibility. Among the professional engineers studied by Gerstl and Hutton (1966), 23 per cent said they had hobbies connected with the field of engineering and as many as 73 per cent claimed work-connected reading as one of their hobby interests.

However, it would be a mistake to suppose that similarity of work and leisure is confined to non-manual and professional employees, though it certainly seems associated with 'service' workers as described in Chapter 5. Thus Shamir (1981) concluded that for hotel workers the distinction between work and non-work is often blurred. They do not treat their work as something to run away from the moment it is finished and their leisure pursuits have much in common with their work.

Heckscher and DeGrazia (1959) concluded from their survey of American business executives that their way of life permits no clear-cut distinction between work and leisure. To counteract the encroachment of work on leisure time, the executive's work is penetrated by qualities which we would ordinarily associate with leisure. But, as Riesman (1952) remarks, the professional or business person is apt to leave his work with a good many tensions created by his reactions to interpersonal situations, and so he may have to satisfy his leisure 'needs' before he can rise from the level of re-creation to the level of creation. He may move from a job where he is constantly faced with others and their expectations to leisure pursuits, again in the company of others, where workmanlike performance is also expected of him.

Another view of executive life is that, though demanding, it need not mean the sacrifice of leisure to work. Willmott's (1971) study of senior staff in London organisations suggests that, though they were much involved in their work, they also had wider than average leisure interests and rather more domestic obligations. This, according to Willmott, calls into question the commonsense belief that involvement in one sphere of life must be at the expense of involvement in another.

The penetration of the businessman's work into the rest of his life is a function of the demands of the work itself rather than of the culture. This is illustrated by the close similarity of the Japanese businessman's life to that of the American's. Vogel (1963) reports that in Japan business is combined with community activities, recreation and personal activities. It is difficult to distinguish working time from leisure time and the businessman often entertains his clients with a trip to the golf course or a party with entertainment by geisha girls. Vogel also notes that, like successful businessmen, doctors rarely make a sharp separation between work and leisure, partly because to some extent working hours are determined by the arrival of patients. It is the salaried man who makes the sharpest distinction between working time and free time. In contrast to the businessman who mixes business and leisure and to the doctor whose leisure is determined by the absence of patients, the salaried man generally has set hours so that he can plan certain hours of the day and certain days of the week for himself and his family.

The type of leisure activity chosen may reflect the type of work and work situation. Even differences in style of a given type of leisure activity may reflect work experiences. Thus Etzkorn (1964) notes that 'public campground' camping, which is routinised, is practised more by individuals with routinised jobs, while 'wilderness' camping is preferred by individuals in more creative occupations. Blum (1953) goes more deeply into the relation between work and leisure experienced by the typical packing-house worker. This type of worker has a tendency to carry work attitudes on into the weekend in spite of a strong psychological fatigue and desire to get away from work and everything it stands for. Since it is almost impossible to work eight hours intensively and switch over suddenly to a new, creative way of life, workers are pushed into some kind of activity which keeps them occupied without reminding them of their work. Fishing is one of their favourite pastimes. It has elements which are just the opposite of the work process – relaxing, being outdoors, getting 'away from it all':

> And yet it has elements akin to the work process. It does not require any initiative or attention and, most of all, it allows the psychological mechanism of busy-ness to go on. It makes it possible to carry an essential attitude growing out of the work process into the

leisure time without making its experience in any way similar to the experience of work ... it eliminates the necessity of a basic change in attitude, of effort and attention. (pp. 109–10)

Types of Work–Leisure Relationship

Three general approaches to the relationship between work and leisure have emerged from empirical research and theorising about the results of such research (Staines, 1980). The first approach asserts a fundamentally positive or similar relationship between work experiences and attitudes on the one hand and leisure experiences and attitudes on the other. I shall generally refer to this as either positive or extension (that is, of the one sphere into the other), although it also appears in the literature as congruence, continuation, convergence, generalisation, identity, integration, isomorphism and spillover. The second approach proposes a negative or dissimilar relationship between work and leisure: one conception of this is opposition but it is also known as compensation, competition, contrast and heteromorphism. Thirdly, the relationship (or, more precisely, lack of relationship) may be designated as one of neutrality or compartmentalisation, segmentation, or separateness.

Types of relationship between work and leisure may be manifested in a number of ways. Some of these, such as expectations and needs satisfied in the two spheres, probably make some contribution to the total explanation of work–leisure relationships, but they have not yet been researched and in our present state of knowledge anything we might say about them would be highly speculative. We can, however, say something with greater confidence about three aspects of the relationship which have been the subject of some research: degree of involvement in work and non-work activities and commitments, types of activities and attitudes to experiences. Each of these aspects – involvement, activities and attitudes – may feature an extension, opposition, or neutral work–leisure relationship and each may relate to one of the other two, for example, work involvement and leisure activities.

(1) *Work involvement related to leisure involvement.* High involvement in work may be positively, negatively, or neutrally related to high involvement in leisure. Considerations favouring the positive relationship include personality type, skills and abilities, and cultural pressures. Some men and women have a general disposition to become involved in all activities, whether work or non-work. Workers heavily involved in their jobs may acquire skills and abilities that facilitate their involvement in non-work activities. And some workers may experience pressures to become involved in social and political activities similar to their work responsibilities (Staines, 1980). In his

study of London architects and Cambridge railwaymen, Salaman (1971) found that such people constitute occupational communities and that their behaviour shows a remarkable convergence of work and non-work. He believes that involvement in work, marginality and restrictive factors are mainly responsible for this convergence.

The negative relationship between involvement in work and in leisure is also exemplified in different ways. One of these assumes that each of us has a fixed amount of 'involvement potential', so that the more time and energy we devote to work activities the less we have to devote to leisure. Another possibility is that we have needs which can be met by involvement in either work or leisure: thus what we get from our experiences at work we do not need to seek outside work, and vice versa (Meissner, 1971).

Thirdly, the neutral relationship between involvement in work and in leisure simply means that time and energy spent in the one sphere has no consequences for time and energy spent in the other. This posits an ability and a desire to segment life spheres which is probably only rarely achieved.

(2) *Work activities related to leisure activities.* A positive relationship is evident when workers choose, consciously or unconsciously, leisure activities that match in character what they do in their work. A negative approach predicts that leisure activities will differ markedly and perhaps intentionally from activities at work. The third possibility is that activities in the two spheres may be unrelated.

The activity component of work–leisure relationships has probably been researched more than any other. Most of the studies support the extension pattern, or what Wilensky (1960) calls 'spillover'. From their study of thirty-two leisure activities of people in eighteen different occupations, Bishop and Ikeda (1970) conclude that those in more masculine occupations tend to participate in more masculine-oriented leisure, while those in feminine occupations tend to choose feminine-oriented leisure. According to Musolino and Hershenon (1977) air traffic controllers with demanding jobs expressed a greater preference for challenging leisure activities than did civil service employees with more routine jobs. The jobs need not be markedly different to show the differential effects on leisure of a significant job-activity component: thus, among workers in similar occupations at the same level of pay, those whose work provides greater autonomy tend to be more 'creative' in their leisure (Torbert and Rogers, 1972). And longitudinal studies show how a change in work activities can be accompanied by a change in leisure activities: Swedish workers whose jobs had become more 'passive' during a six-year period became more passive in their leisure, while workers with more 'active' jobs became more active (Karasek, 1981).

In a summary review, Cheek and Burch (1976) conclude that 'there seems most support for the spillover, or congruence, hypothesis that nonwork activities are similar to work activities'. However, a few studies lend support to the idea that work and leisure activities tend to be unlike each other. The pioneer theorising by Wilensky (1960) pointed to compensation as an alternative theme to spillover from work to leisure activities, including 'explosive compensation for the deadening rhythms of factory life'. Kando and Summers (1971) subsequently suggested that there are two types of compensation: supplemental, when desirable work features not present in the work situation are sought in leisure, and reactive, when undesirable work features are 'corrected' in the leisure context.

Chisholm's (1978) research among junior to mid-level management employees suggests that, although their feelings of alienation carry over strongly from work to leisure, only limited carry-over occurs between job activities and those away from work. And Gardell's (1976) study of sawmill workers shows that physically demanding work activities can inhibit similar leisure activities. Many such workers are too tired even to speak to wives and children for several hours after arriving home, because it takes that long for the noise and machine-paced tempo of the mill to vanish from mind and body. It may be, however, that compensation is a dominant theme in the leisure lives mainly of those with physically demanding jobs. Certainly Kelly (1976) found compensatory elements were rare in the leisure choices of a general sample of workers in an industrial town.

All the studies which link similarity or dissimilarity of work and leisure activities to specific occupations or types of work should not lead us to neglect differences arising from personal values. As Kando (1975) reminds us, possibilities of both compensation and spillover exist regardless of a person's occupation. Two individuals with the same job, say, for instance, college professors, may prefer different leisure activities; one may feel physical deprivation and therefore engage in athletics (compensation), while the other, feeling no such deprivation, spends more of his leisure time reading and writing (spillover).

(3) *Work attitudes related to leisure attitudes.* Again, the three possible values of the relationship are positive, negative and neutral. Much, but by no means all, of the evidence supports the proposition that attitudes in one sphere carry over to the other and that this more often occurs from work to leisure than vice versa. Thus Orpen's (1978) results from an inquiry among seventy-three South African managers indicate that the direction of causality from work to non-work satisfaction is stronger than that in the opposite direction. However, Rice and his colleagues (1979) conclude from a New York sample of 1,041

people that extra-work variables such as life satisfaction can have an impact on job satisfaction quite apart from the influence of work-related variables.

Rousseau (1978) reports a positive correlation between job satisfaction and satisfaction with life outside work, among a predominantly female sample. By contrast, a study by Spreitzer and Snyder (1974) lends support to the compensation hypothesis: they conclude that those deriving few satisfactions from their jobs are likely to report leisure as the major area of self-identification; and the neutrality hypothesis is favoured by London and his colleagues (1977), who studied the contribution of job and leisure satisfaction to the quality of life and conclude that most people seem to segment their experiences, so that feelings derived from work and leisure are basically unrelated. This is supported by the findings of Gupta and Beehr (1981) that, in general, employee reactions in the work and non-work spheres are dissimilar.

Apart from satisfaction, attitudes which are positive towards work may be allied to those which are negative towards leisure. Allen and Hawes (1979) obtained data from a sample of the general United States population on attitudes towards work, leisure and the four-day workweek, and found that those who favoured the shorter work-week, as compared with those who did not, were significantly more leisure-oriented (see Table 7.1).

Table 7.1   *Attitudes to the 4-Day Workweek*

	Favour (N = 309) %	Do not favour (N = 132) %
I would not work if I did not have to	55	22
I express my talents better in my leisure activities than in my job	47	32
I have enough leisure time	14	36

(4) *Other relationships between work and leisure variables.* Staines (1980) notes that, in addition to the three paired relationships considered above, there are three other possible cross-relationships: (1) involvement-activities, (2) involvement-attitudes and (3) activities-attitudes. Each of the terms can relate either to work or to leisure and each of the paired terms can (at least theoretically) show positive, negative, or neutral relationships.

However, research on work–leisure relationships has been fragmented and has not proceeded within this or any other framework. So we have, to date, accumulated only some patchy results, often indeterminate and with many questions left unanswered.

As an example of relationship between work attitudes and leisure activities we may take the research by Grubb (1975) on car assembly-line work. He hypothesised that people doing more boring jobs would increase their leisure activity, but found few differences in the activities undertaken by any group. It seemed that structural influences, such as working a six-day week, governed their leisure participation rather than feelings about the job.

In a more general analysis of work and leisure relationships than most of the research reported above, Kabanoff and O'Brien (1980) use the concept of 'task attributes' to delineate the features of both work and leisure, which they take to be influence, variety, pressure, skill utilisation and interaction. Using low–high categories of work and leisure attributes, they isolate four groups: passive generalisation (people low on both work and leisure attributes), supplemental compensation (low work, high leisure), active generalisation (high on both) and reactive compensation (high work, low leisure). From their research on a sample of the Australian working population, they conclude that there is only a weak relationship between work and leisure attributes. They suggest that, rather than ask 'how does work determine leisure?', it would be more fruitful to ask 'which factors are associated with, or cause people to have, different work/leisure patterns?', or 'how do people balance their commitment across different life spheres?'

The Rapoports (1975) give a different example of a situation in which it is meaningless to talk about work determining leisure or vice versa. One of their case studies is of Tom, a young musician. His work and non-work activities are identical. He and his friends are totally immersed in establishing their music group and in attempting to find audiences. To Tom, 'leisure' is 'doing just what you want to be doing – playing music, getting stoned, being with people you like to be with'. Once he came to enjoy his work, he found it meaningless to distinguish 'free time' from 'work'. Some of the residential social workers I studied (see Chapter 5) gave the same message.

With such examples in mind of a high degree of integration of work and leisure, the Rapoports question how far many of our conventional views of the work–leisure relationship still hold good. Some people have a clear part of their lives that is work (which may be positively or negatively defined) and a clear part that is leisure. But for increasing numbers of people this model may not hold. Rather, there are degrees of clarity in the definition between work and non-work interests: degrees of 'porosity' in the work situation, during which leisure-like enjoyment may be experienced and degrees of flexibility in the dispersion of work into other situations.

The idea that leisure can be experienced in work is consistent with what we know about the nature of satisfying activities. As Argyle (1972) points out, work should have many of the properties of leisure to be most satisfying and the converse is also true. People will seek certain activities, whether they are called work or leisure, because they fulfil the conditions for human satisfaction: completing interesting and meaningful tasks, which use basic skills and abilities, giving adequate recognition and social status.

The research findings we have considered so far in this section have contributed to our greater understanding of the relationship between work and leisure. Some of the inquiries have been based on more or less explicit theories about the nature of this relationship, but before attempting an assessment of progress towards a theory of work–leisure relationships, I propose to deal with two other matters that affect the relationship in question: central life interest and fusion of work and leisure versus polarity.

Central Life Interest

We can learn much about the nature of the relationship between work and leisure from the relative values which people place on these two spheres of life. Dubin (1956) has coined the term 'central life interest' to refer to an expressed preference for a given locale or situation in carrying out an activity. Assuming that social participation in a sphere may be necessary but not important to an individual, he classified replies by industrial workers to a series of three-choice questions as job-oriented, non job-oriented, or indifferent. He did this separately for questions concerning formal (organisational), technical and informal dimensions of work experience.

The results showed that, by a margin of three to one, work was not in general a central life interest for the industrial workers sampled, although the detailed analysis revealed that work rather than non-work locales were preferred by a majority in regard to formal and technical experiences. He concluded that, while many industrial workers become attached to impersonal work features, few are attached to work by virtue of their social relationships with fellow workers. Such a conclusion, however, is open to question. It implies that 'impersonal work features' are superficial in the lives of workers and that the deeper meaning of 'social relationships' is found outside the work situation. But questionnaire answers may be misleading, as Goodman (1962) points out:

What the men are apparently interested in is time off the job; they are just waiting for the whistle to blow so they can get to their 'important' interests; but strangely, these important life interests are *not* directive, controlling, rewarding; they are not the areas of learning how to belong and how to avoid being excluded. Such things are rather learned on the job, in which, however, they are not interested! (p. 450)

These findings, it should be noted, apply to industrial workers and Dubin and his colleagues (1976) report subsequent studies of similar groups of workers showing the same general pattern. But they also report on findings of central life interest research carried out among other types of worker, such as managers and professional employees. For example, Orzack's (1959) results with professional nurses confirmed his prediction that professionals would be much more oriented to work as a central life interest than would industrial workers. By nearly four to one the nurses gave overall 'work' replies and only in the case of informal relations was the non-work sphere slightly preferred.

Other central life interest research, using different questions from those of Dubin and his colleagues, has focused mainly on manual workers. Kornhauser (1965) reported that the job was chosen as the most satisfying part of life by only 2 per cent of routine production workers compared with 9 per cent of other factory men. Lafitte (1958) found that the engagements into which Australian factory workers put their major efforts varied considerably, but were chiefly outside work. The worker, he concluded, may be family-centred or self- centred, but he is never work-centred. Dumazedier (1967) asked a sample of French workers in the town of Annecy which activities gave them most satisfaction. Of unskilled workers, 25 per cent replied 'leisure', 47 per cent 'family' and 24 per cent 'work'. Of skilled workers, 25 per cent replied 'leisure', 53 per cent 'family' and only 15 per cent 'work'.

A study going more deeply into the central life interest of various types of industrial worker is reported by Odaka (1966). Five Japanese companies were included in the survey, which involved several thousand employees. Respondents were asked to choose from a list of items the one which they felt contributed most to making their life worth living. The most popular answer was 'making a happy home' (36–56 per cent), followed by 'leisure' (25–47 per cent), with 'work at the company' a poor third (6–14 per cent). Another question sought to classify workers' preferences among 'five types of living related to work and leisure'. These were defined as:

1 Work-oriented-unilateral – 'Work is man's duty. I wish to devote myself wholly to my work without any thought of leisure.'

Table 7.2   *Type of Work–Leisure Relationship*

	(1) Work-oriented-unilateral %	(2) Leisure-oriented-unilateral %	(3) Identity %	(4) Split %	(5) Integrated %	Others and Unknown %	Total %
Temporary operative	15	12	15	18	38	3	101
Regular operative	8	5	8	25	53	1	100
Supervisory	18	3	5	24	49	2	101
Administrative	22	4	4	22	48	—	100
Technical	23	7	7	7	55	2	101
Whole company	12	5	7	23	51	2	100

2   Leisure-oriented-unilateral – 'Work is no more than a means for living. The enjoyment of leisure is what makes human life worth living.'
3   Identity – 'There is no distinction between work and leisure. I therefore have no need of being liberated from work in order that I may enjoy leisure.'
4   Split – 'Work is work and leisure is leisure. Modern man gets his work done smartly, and enjoys his leisure moderately.'
5   Integrated – 'Work makes leisure pleasurable, and leisure gives new energy to work. I wish to work with all my might, and to enjoy leisure.'

The replies of more than 600 employees in one manufacturing company were analysed according to their type of work in the company (see Table 7.2). With one or two exceptions, the distribution of replies according to type of work was fairly similar. It must be borne in mind, however, that all the respondents were in one company and this may have had the effect of narrowing differences which a survey including a wider range of occupations might have revealed. Certainly the majority verdict in favour of the 'integrated' pattern – confirmed in a later Japanese study (*Fuji Bank Bulletin*, 1972) – seems to conflict with the much more popular choice of non-work rather than work as what makes life worth living.

Fusion versus Polarity

The type of relationship existing between work and leisure spheres is to be seen at both the societal and the individual level. We may first consider the arguments for and against the proposition that work and leisure are becoming similar to each other. At the societal level the evidence for both 'fusion' and 'polarity' consists of changes that have allegedly taken place in the content of work, the way it is organised and the setting in which it is done. At the individual level, fusion would be experienced as spillover of work and leisure spheres and polarity as opposition, or at least differentiation, of these spheres.

Wilensky (1964) cites as evidence of work–leisure fusion the long coffee break among white-collar girls, the lunch 'hour' among top business and professional people, card games among night shift employees; and off work, the do-it-yourself movement, spare-time jobs, 'customer's golf' for sales executives and commuter-train conferences for account executives. Also, many devices are being invented to create spaces of free time within the working day and at intervals throughout the career. In America the sabbatical year is no longer exclusive to academic employees. One firm has for some time been granting twelve months' paid holiday after ten years of service, and other employees have the chance of a quarter-sabbatical – three months off after five years' service (Klausner, 1968). Another type of work-leisure fusion, the integration of sex into work, is noted by Marcuse (1964): 'Without ceasing to be an instrument of labor, the body is allowed to exhibit its sexual features in the everyday work world and in work relations.' A negative feature of this development is an apparent increase in the incidence of sexual harassment at the workplace.

No doubt with such evidence as this in mind, Stone (1958) has asserted that

> more and more we work at our play and play at our work ... our play is disguised by work and vice versa. Consequently, we begin to evaluate our leisure time in terms of the potential it has for work – for us to 'do it ourselves', and we evaluate our work in terms of the potential it has for play. (p. 285)

The people whose leisure assumes the character of 'anti-leisure' – compulsive, constrained, time-conscious activity (Godbey, 1975) – are another example of how work and leisure can interpenetrate.

Riesman (1953) attempts to explain this work–leisure fusion in terms of the 'changing American character' from inner-directedness to other-directedness: 'The other-directed person has no clear core of self to escape from; no clear line between production and consumption; between adjusting to the group and serving private interests; between work and play.' Yet other-directedness is not so much a type of character as a mode of adjustment to technological civilisation. The aspect of leisure that is most amenable to fusion with work is mass culture, because it is most subject to social control and therefore can be made most 'functional' to the industrial system as a whole. Howe (1948) saw this process of manipulation clearly:

> Except during brief revolutionary intervals, the quality of leisure time activity cannot vary too sharply from that of the work day. If it did, the office or factory worker would be exposed to those terrible dualities that make it so difficult for the intellectual to adjust his job to himself. But the worker wants no part of such difficulties, he has enough already. Following the dictum of industrial society that anonymity is a key to safety, he seeks the least troublesome solution: mass culture. Whatever its manifest content, mass culture must therefore not subvert the basic patterns of industrial life. Leisure time must be so organized as to bear a factitious relationship to working time: apparently different, actually the same. It must provide relief from work monotony without making the return to work too unbearable. (p. 120)

The popular game of bingo is a good example. Bingo has several features which are similar to the work experience of many of those who take part in it: it involves concentration and regulated patterns of physical movement, is supervised by someone else and allows breaks for refreshments.

There are other observers, however, who take a different view about what has been happening to work and leisure. Dismissing evidence of fusion such as that cited above as marginal to the main structure of modern industry, they seek to show that work has become more concentratedly and actively work. It may be less arduous physically than it used to be, but its present standards of efficiency are said to require one to key oneself to a higher pitch of nervous and mental effort. The theme of alienation from work is relevant here, since it implies that work as a sphere of human experience is estranged from other spheres such as leisure. Under conditions of present society, it is said, the 'break in consciousness' between work and socialised play, begun during the Industrial Revolution, has been completed. Certainly it is arguable that the institution of employment has brought about a fairly sharp distinction between working life and private life, between sold time and unsold time. The 'evasion of work', according to Daniel Bell (1954), is the characteristic fact about work in the life of a contemporary American:

> Work is irksome, and if it cannot be evaded it can be reduced. In the old days the shadings between work and leisure were hard to

distinguish. In modern life the ideal is to minimize the unpleasant aspects of work as much as possible by pleasant distractions (wall colors, music, rest periods) and to hasten away as quickly as possible, uncontaminated by work and unimpaired by its arduousness. (p. 20)

The ideal may be to split the unsatisfying life of work from the more rewarding life of non-work, but we must reserve judgement on the extent to which this ideal is actually being achieved.

The evidence for fusion or polarity of work and leisure at the societal level is conflicting and the theories built on selections from this evidence are not easily reconcilable. Perhaps the whole argument has been confused by referring to different levels – that of society in general and that of occupations and work *milieux* in particular – each of which requires its own methods of analysis and conclusions. Also, fusion and polarity may not exhaust all the possibilities of relationship between work and leisure. The concepts of fusion and polarity are essentially dynamic ones referring to a process of change in a relationship. They also denote symbiotic relationships, in the sense that each side of the relationship is dependent for its form on the form of the other – by a process, as it were, of positive attraction or negative repulsion. This leaves a third possibility: that the nature of the relationship between work and leisure may be non-symbiotic, that is, that work and leisure may each have 'lives of their own' and be relatively unaffected by each other.

It is this third possibility which no doubt motivates some sceptics of the real extent of work influences on leisure. Thus Roberts and his colleagues (1976)

question the utility of conceptualising leisure as a part of life mainly ancillary to work, to be understood in terms of the degree to which it is complementary to, the opposite of, or an extension of occupational life. While this perspective contains some validity, we are sceptical of efforts to treat it as of central importance in the study of leisure behaviour. (p. 29)

Having examined the relevant research, I agree that work–leisure relationships are not the only important feature of the study of leisure, but, though complex, they are certainly one of the most important.

8
Towards a Theory of Work and Leisure

There are broadly two schools of thought about the relationship between spheres of life in our present type of urban-industrial society. The first (whose adherents may be called segmentalists) hold that people's lives are split into different areas of activity and interest, with each social segment lived out more or less independently of the rest. Work, they say, is separated from leisure, production from consumption, workplace from residence, education from religion, politics from recreation. The second school (the holists) maintain that society is essentially an integrated whole, every part of which affects and is affected by every other part. Attitudes and practices developed in one sphere of life, they say, can spill over into another – killing time at work can become killing time in leisure, apathy in the workplace can become apathy in politics, alienation from the one can become alienation from the other.

These holist and segmentalist schools of thought about society as a whole may be related to the arguments of the supporters of fusion or polarity as explanations of trends in the relationship between work and leisure. The evidence for fusion and polarity was considered in Chapter 7 and found to be inconclusive when considering society as a whole. With holism and segmentalism, however, it is not so much a matter of weighing up evidence as of accepting or rejecting a philosophy of life.

Each of us has a philosophy of life, whether or not we consciously think about it. In considering the ways in which work and leisure pose problems for us in our own lives we tend to adopt one outlook rather than another. The sort of solutions we prescribe for ourselves or for other people stem from the particular philosophy we hold. Whether these prescribed solutions 'work', whether they can be put into practice, depends on how closely they fit the conditions and trends in our society or community.

The alternative philosophies of holism and segmentalism have implications for the integration of the individual in society. With the segmentalist view, the individual may be seen as obliged to pick and choose, to divide his loyalties and to become what McClung Lee (1966) has called 'multivalent man', changing his social self to fit in with the values of the groups he belongs to as he moves from one to another. A rigid application of the holist view would mean seeing the essential unity of society and of culture as leading to a danger of decline in the creative autonomy of the individual, a general sense of oppression and a feeling that there is no escape from the total pattern of life to which we find ourselves committed. But, as Godbey (1981) believes, a holistic approach to work and leisure may be a matter of integrating them more through faith than through changing the constraints of work and making it more like leisure. Both segmentalism and holism appear to be valid to some extent when we consider society as a whole and the concern, when we consider smaller groups or individuals, is to determine when work and leisure can be experienced as separate and often opposed spheres, and when the character of the one can usefully spill over into the other.

If we assume that work, in its most creative forms, fulfils certain human needs, we may ask what happens to these needs when the quality of working life is too poor to fulfil them. Most jobs today are regarded by the mass of people only as a means to the end of earning a living. Many workers find their real sense of satisfaction from things they do and people they mix with after they leave the workplace. This does not necessarily mean that satisfaction is found outside work itself, defined in wider terms than paid employment. For some men and women the need for creative expression of workmanship flourishes in leisure, in do-it-yourself work, the care of cars or gardens, the 'inventive puttering of life after work'.

Levels and Patterns

There are two levels on which we may consider the various possible types of relationship between work and leisure: in the life of the individual and in the structure of the society in which he lives. This, in fact, oversimplifies the matter because there are levels intermediate between the individual and the societal (for instance, the group), but the analysis is clearer if confined to these two levels and to a general description of the type of relationship (see Table 8.1). These general descriptions are the broadest possible ways in which we can look at work and leisure, covering both individuals and the society of which they are part. *Identity* describes any situation where work and leisure feature similar structures, behaviour, or purposes. *Contrast* means a definition of the content of one sphere as the absence or opposite of the other. *Separateness* sums up a situation of minimal contact or influence between the spheres. It will be helpful to remember these general

Table 8.1   *Types of Work–Leisure Relationship*

General description	Individual level	Societal level
identity	extension	fusion
contrast	opposition	polarity
separateness	neutrality	containment

descriptions when considering the different types of relationship between work and leisure and the important question of whether there is a connection between the two levels.

First, however, I shall consider the proposition that there are three main types of relationship between work and leisure and that each of us tends to have one of these in his own pattern of life. I introduced in Chapter 5 the terms 'extension', 'opposition' and 'neutrality' to describe the various types of relationship between occupation and council work for local government councillors. Now we can see how far these terms may be used to group together the patterns of work and leisure shown by the other types of people mentioned. The *extension* pattern consists of having leisure activities which are often similar in content to one's working activities and of making no sharp distinction between what is considered as work and what as leisure. With the *opposition* pattern, leisure activities are deliberately unlike work and there is a sharp distinction between what is work and what is leisure. Finally, the *neutrality* pattern consists of having leisure activities which are generally different from work but not deliberately so, and of appreciating the difference between work and leisure without always defining the one as the absence of the other.

Before going on to examine these individual patterns of work–leisure relationship in detail, we may look briefly at their equivalents at the societal level. Extension of work into leisure (and vice versa) in the life of the person is paralleled by fusion of the work and leisure spheres in society as a whole. Individual opposition of work and leisure is matched by polarity of the spheres in society. Individual neutrality between work and leisure is matched by containment of the spheres in society. This is not to say that the societal arrangements for work and leisure necessarily impose themselves on every aspect of our personal lives. But it is obviously easier to sustain a personal pattern that is in line with the pattern of society, or at least of that part of society in which we move. For example, if we want to keep work and leisure as distinctly opposite parts of our lives we shall find this easier to do in a society that keeps places of work free from the influence of leisure and places of leisure free from the taint of work.

Returning to work–leisure relationships at the individual level, first these need careful definition. Then I shall look at the aspects of occupations and work involvement ('work variables') that seem to be associated with each of these patterns of relationship. Finally, I shall deal with the non-work (mainly leisure) variables that are also associated with the patterns. In this way it is possible to build up a total picture of what it means to have an extension, opposition, or neutrality pattern of work and leisure.

In Table 8.2 the details are set out in summary form. The various descriptions of values of the variables are based on research conclusions already noted in earlier chapters, but sometimes a certain amount of speculation is involved. Further research may require that some of the details be changed or qualified.

Table 8.2   *Types of Work–Leisure Relationship and Associated Variables (Individual Level)*

Work–leisure relationship variables	Extension	Opposition	Neutrality
Content of work and leisure	similar	deliberately different	usually different
Demarcation of spheres	weak	strong	average
Central life interest	work	—	non-work
Imprint left by work on leisure	marked	marked	not marked
Work variables			
Autonomy in work situation	high	—	low
Use of abilities (how far extended)	fully ('stretched')	uneven ('damaged')	little or no ('bored')
Involvement	moral	alienative	calculative
Work colleagues	include some close friends	—	include no close friends
Work encroachment on leisure	high	low	low
Typical occupations	social workers (especially residential)	'extreme' (mining, fishing)	routine clerical and manual
Non-work variables			
Educational level	high	low	medium
Duration of leisure	short	irregular	long
Main function of leisure	continuation of personal development	recuperation	entertainment

To put some flesh on the bare bones of Table 8.2 we may consider just what it means in human terms to have each of these patterns. With extension there is a similarity between at least some work and leisure activities and a lack of demarcation between what is called work and what is called leisure. The extreme cases of people having this pattern are those who are free from the necessity of earning a living but who do work of a kind and in circumstances of their choice. A larger group of people includes those whose lives show a strong tendency to extension of work into leisure but also some elements of opposition and/or neutrality. Thus some social workers feel that it is bad for them and for their clients if they are too work-centred, and their leisure accordingly has some elements of deliberate opposition to work. Having work as a central life interest is part of the definition of the extension pattern. This is because work, to someone who sees a continuity between work and leisure, is a much more embracing concept than just 'the job' or even 'the occupation'. Work signifies the meaning and fulfilment of life, and in saying that it is also the centre of life such people are not necessarily denying the integrated role that leisure plays in it. Also, because of deep involvement in their kind of work it leaves a relatively great imprint on the rest of their lives – it is often an influence from which they are never really free.

The key aspects of the opposition pattern are the intention dissimilarity of work and leisure, and the strong demarcation between the two spheres. The extreme cases of this pattern are those who hate their work so much that any reminder of it in their off-duty time is unpleasant. But paradoxically such people do not in one sense get away from work at all: so deeply are they marked by the hated experience of work that they measure the delights of leisure according to how much unlike work they are. Thus if work means submission to authority then leisure means 'having a go' at authority in some other way. A less pure type of opposition between work and leisure is shown by the person who has an ambivalent rather than a completely hostile attitude to work – he hates it because of the physical or psychological damage that he feels it does to him, yet he 'loves' it because he is fascinated by its arduousness or by its dangers (it is 'real man's work'). The strain of such work ensures that it is not carried over into leisure, from which it is clearly demarcated. With opposition, the source of central life interest is generally not clear; if work is viewed with unmixed hatred then presumably non-work is seen as the centre of life, but if there is a love-hate relationship to work then either sphere could be seen as central, or perhaps the very opposition and dissimilarity of the spheres renders the person incapable of making a comparative judgement.

The third pattern of neutrality is only partly defined by a 'usually different' content of work and leisure and by an 'average' demarcation of spheres. This pattern is in many ways not intermediate between the extension and opposition patterns, although it may at first glance appear to be so. The crucial difference between extension and opposition on the one hand, and neutrality on the other, is that the former denote respectively a positive and negative attachment to work, while the latter denotes a detachment from work that is, in Berger's (1964) phrase, neither fulfilment nor oppression. With extension and opposition the imprint left by work on leisure is relatively marked, in either a positive or negative way. But people showing the neutrality pattern are neither so engrossed in their work that they want to carry it over into non-work time nor so damaged by it that they develop a hostile or love-hate relation to it. Instead, work leaves them comparatively unmarked and free to carry over into leisure the non-involvement and passivity which characterises their attitude to work. In other words, detachment from any real responsibility for and interest in work tends to lead to detachment from any active and constructive leisure pursuits. Although some individuals are able to break out of this vicious circle, the tendency is to sit back and wait to be entertained. Since entertainment is more 'fun' than work, people with the neutrality pattern are likely to find their central life interest outside the work sphere.

Associated Variables

Turning now to the work variables associated with the three patterns, we may note first the effect of degree of autonomy in the work situation. The study of social workers with relatively high autonomy showed that they were also very likely to exhibit the extension pattern. But the bank workers, who generally had little autonomy, typically showed the neutrality pattern. The conclusion for the opposition pattern is not so clear. Autonomy is probably low for most of these people, being accompanied by little interest in the work itself and hence a desire to escape from it. But a highly individualistic work situation, neither machine-paced nor closely supervised, could also be accompanied by opposition of work and leisure if the attitude to work were one of alienation.

The second work variable, use of abilities, needs to be analysed in terms of both amount and evenness of being extended or 'used' in the job. The social workers, who used most of their abilities in an intensive way, tended to show the extension pattern, while the bank workers, usually less extended in their jobs, tended to show the neutrality pattern. Those men and women who are unevenly extended in their jobs are likely to want to compensate for this by a counterbalancing type of non-work life that will help to repair the ravages of work. To sum up on use of abilities, we can say that extension is usually accompanied by a feeling of being 'stretched' by the work, neutrality by being 'bored' with it, and opposition by being 'damaged' by it.

To describe types of involvement in work we may draw upon Etzioni's (1961) types of involvement by 'lower participants' in organisations – moral, calculative and alienative. Since we are restricting our analysis to economic (employing) organisations and do not, as Etzioni does, include a comparison of economic with other kinds of organisation, the parallel is not an exact one; it may nevertheless be worth making. Accepting that economic reward is a motive common to all employees for participating in work organisations, we may describe as 'moral' the kind of involvement which produces a desire to go on working in that way even if freed from the necessity of earning a living. 'Calculative' involvement occurs where the work is done consciously as part of a transaction, that is, where economic reward is overwhelmingly the main motivation. 'Alienative' involvement occurs where economic reward is also important but is experienced less as a transaction than as a sense of being forced to do the job against one's will. These three types of involvement seem to be associated respectively with the extension, neutrality and opposition patterns of work and leisure, although these is some ambiguity between the last two patterns.

The likelihood of having some work colleagues among one's close friends is high among those with the extension pattern and low among those with the neutrality pattern. Again, the opposition people are not so predictable. If work is hated then presumably the thought of mixing with work colleagues off the job is also hateful (and this may help to explain the feeling among some factory workers that 'mating is not palling'), but it is also possible that the damaging experience of work is made more tolerable by a feeling of solidarity with workmates whose company may well be sought off the job. An 'occupational community' does not require that all members be positively involved in the work: all may be negatively involved, provided that they are conscious of sharing this feeling.

The degree of encroachment of work on leisure is high for those with the extension pattern and low for the other two groups. The extension people are likely to let their work carry over into leisure time because they find it interesting for its own sake. Where work does encroach on the leisure time of the neutrality group, it is likely to do so only as a means to an end, for example, to pass examinations in order to get promotion. Where work encroaches on the leisure time of the opposition group, it does so only in the sense that a person must first recover from the effects of this kind of work before he can enjoy leisure.

The above analysis of work variables in relation to types of work–leisure relationship has been based on the research reported in earlier chapters. This research has mostly been concerned with specific occupational groups, although the effects of certain variables within occupational groups have also been noted. I do not claim that certain occupations and certain types of work–leisure relationship always go together, but to round off the discussion of work variables the following tentative additions may be made to the typical occupations listed in Table 8.2. Extension may also include successful businessmen (perhaps they are successful because they have little or no time for leisure), doctors, teachers and self-employed workers; neutrality may include minor professionals other than social workers; and opposition may cover unskilled manual workers, assembly-line workers, oil rig workers and tunnellers (the last two being 'extreme' occupations in the sense both of high pay and physical working conditions).

We now come to three non-work variables – one of education and two of leisure. Concerning education, the child care officers, the majority of whom showed the extension pattern, also had, in the majority, attended university. The bank employees, the majority of whom showed the neutrality pattern, had mostly attended grammar schools but had not gone on to higher education. The large majority of the 'opposition' manual workers had had only elementary or secondary modern education. The question arises: is it type of education which determines the occupation which in turn influences work–leisure patterns, or does education exert an influence on work–leisure patterns independently of occupation? There are two clues to the answer to this difficult question. One is my own impression gained from the pilot interviews with business and service workers. Several of the people in business occupations who had a neutrality work–leisure pattern had been well educated (university or public school) yet seemed far less involved in their work than some of the less well-educated social workers who had an extension pattern. Secondly, the analysis of attitudes of local government councillors suggests that a number of manual-worker councillors had been so 'educated' by their experience of public work that they now felt capable of doing things which they felt they would have been prevented from doing previously by their low level of formal education. Both of these clues point in the direction of the influence of work experience on work–leisure patterns independently of the level of formal education.

There is ample evidence that professional and business employees have less time for leisure than the mass of routine and clerical workers

(Linder, 1970). This suggests 'short' and 'long' duration of leisure time for those with the extension and neutrality patterns respectively. Again, the opposition pattern presents problems. The distant-water fishermen have about nine months of the year at sea and three months ashore, mostly as leisure time; the latter, therefore, is better described as 'irregular' rather than as either long or short. For others with the opposition pattern the lack of work encroachment on leisure may mean a relatively long duration of leisure, but a willingness to work long hours for big money would shorten available leisure time. There is, then, no general conclusion about duration of leisure time for those with the opposition pattern.

Finally, there is the question of the main function of leisure. Here it seems reasonable to borrow and modify slightly Dumazedier's (1967) three functions of personal development, entertainment and relaxation to apply to extension, neutrality and opposition respectively. For 'personal development' we may substitute 'continuation of personal development', since the work done by people with the extension pattern is usually of the kind that promotes personal development and the need is for leisure to continue it in a different or complementary way. 'Entertainment' has the right connotation of relief from boredom to describe the function of 'neutrality' leisure. 'Relaxation', however, is too similar to, and implies too much of the passivity of, entertainment to describe 'opposition' leisure, and the term 'recuperation' seems preferable. It should be understood that only in exceptional cases does any one of these three functions characterise the whole of leisure. For example, we may say that a person has the extension pattern because the general nature of the relationship between his work and his leisure is as outlined in Table 8.2, but that need not stop him from sometimes feeling the need for recuperation or entertainment.

Subsequent Criticisms and Refinements

Since my original formulation of the three work–leisure relationships there have been a number of critical assessments of these, which in turn have led me to some revisions to meet those criticisms which seem to be justified. In reviewing models, methods and findings in work and non-work research, Kabanoff (1980) sees our aim as

> to describe different work/leisure/family patterns, to discover the factors that determine these patterns, and to relate these patterns to other significant life outcomes such as general life satisfaction, work and leisure satisfaction, physical and mental health, and so on. (p. 74)

It seems that we are not so far advanced in this endeavour as to be able to be dogmatic about any statements we venture to make or to ignore constructive criticisms of those statements.

Clayre (1974) says of my typology that

> it leaves many questions open. It is a classification of people's activities only. But people do not necessarily find either the work or leisure they want; so their needs and wishes cannot necessarily be assessed from their actions. There may be more people seeking 'extension' or 'compensation' in leisure than actually finding it. (p. 198)

Although my typology certainly focuses on activities, it does so very much in the context of the functions of those activities in the life pattern rather than being concerned simply with the content of the activities. Clayre is right to claim that needs and wishes cannot always be assessed from actions – or even from personal statements. I am not even sure that it is valid to say that people are seeking extension or compensation. Many would no doubt like their work to be as interesting and creative as their leisure (and a few vice versa), while others are aware that mass-produced and passive leisure does not make up for work with the same limiting characteristics. If social scientists are to become social commentators and hence agents of social change, then they will have to find ways of encouraging people to regard as problematic and alterable what they now see as inevitable and beyond their control.

Bacon (1972a), in the course of a critical review of concepts used in research on work–leisure relationships, suggests that these relationships may be examined on two dimensions: behavioural, which concerns the degree of fusion or polarity between the component elements of leisure and work; and normative, the degree to which values found in the work sphere complement or are opposed to values in the leisure sphere. Bacon's own research (1975) on hobbyist craftworkers and his assessment of other research of a similar nature leads him to conclude that there is little evidence of behavioural relationships between work and leisure but some evidence of normative relationships: 'To a considerable extent, the things that people choose to do in their free time are unrelated to the nature of their employment.' But he readily acknowledges that my types of work–leisure relationship (which he amends for measurement purposes to low, medium and high work-generated alienation) correlate well with various statements about fusion, opposition and neutrality between work and leisure. For example, 52 per cent of his craftworkers with high work-generated alienation, but only 15 per cent with low alienation, said 'I put up with my work and do the things that really interest me in my leisure' (Bacon, 1977).

Although Bacon does not specifically disagree with my hypothesis that people with different types of work–leisure relationship will tend to have different main functions of leisure (exemplified by continuation of personal development, recuperation and entertainment), his research suggests that these 'functions' need to be interpreted carefully. He found that his hobbyist craftworkers, who had a variety of occupations and who fell into three different work–leisure relationship groups similar to mine, differed little in either their reasons for taking up craftwork as a hobby or their evaluation of the benefits they received from this leisure activity. Roughly equal proportions in all work–leisure relationship groups expressed a desire to produce tangible and useful products, to be creative and imaginative, and so on.

I see Bacon's results as warning us not to imagine that a particular leisure activity, such as craftwork, tends to be taken up mainly by people with one type of work–leisure relationship. But the predominantly 'neutralist' routine clerical workers who take up craftwork are probably not representative, in terms of the main function of their leisure, of the generality of routine clerical workers. Research which looks at the whole range of leisure activities and functions of 'neutralist' routine clerical workers may well find that more of them simply want to be entertained and have nothing to do with things like craftwork as compared with other occupational and work–leisure relationship groups.

Roberts (1974) quite rightly insists that work–leisure relationships should be distinguished at the individual and societal levels and in behavioural and ideational terms.

> At the level of individuals' life-styles, leisure interests are often only weakly related to characteristics of people's jobs, though types of work do have some bearing upon leisure interests... But individuals with similar jobs can cultivate completely dissimilar leisure tastes. Conversely, people with quite different jobs may choose to spend their free time in similar ways. (p. 27)

This line of reasoning is consistent with Bacon's findings on craftworkers. Distinguishing ideas from behaviour is important because relationships discovered between work and leisure at one level will not necessarily be reflected at the other. As Roberts notes, leisure could be more potent than work in giving meaning to life, while job factors could be stronger in influencing leisure behaviour. In a similar vein, Mansfield and Evans (1975) suggest a distinction between the form and meaning of a person's activities both in and out of work.

We are still some way from being able to make confident and reasonably reliable statements about the complex web of different dimensions of the work–leisure relationship. As Near and his colleagues (1980) remark, in order to determine actual relationships between work and non-work thoroughly developed conceptual models must be devised and more sophisticated design and data analysis procedures must be used. We have so far assembled some fairly reliable statistical associations between attitudes to work and other domains of life, but we do not yet know much about the pathways underlying such relationships, their direction of causality, or relative strength.

Philosophical Implications

It now remains to relate what was said earlier in this chapter about the philosophies of segmentalism and holism to the general (individual and societal) types of work–leisure relationship. This means trying to find a connection between how people think about the world (society and themselves), how the societal spheres of work and leisure are related, and how the work and leisure parts of their lives are related. The suggested parallels are set out in Table 8.3.

Table 8.3   *The Connection between Philosophies and Work–Leisure Relationships*

Philosophy	Work–leisure relationship
Holism	Identity
Segmentalism	{ Contrast / Separateness

A person who sees that the parts of his life are integrated, each one affecting and being affected by the others (holism), is likely to have an extension pattern of work and leisure and to live in a society – or at least in a social circle – in which the spheres of work and leisure are relatively fused (identity). On the other hand, a person who sees the parts of his life as separate segments comparatively unaffected by each other (segmentalism) is unlikely to have either of the other two types of work–leisure relationship. Either he will have an opposition pattern of work and leisure and most likely live in a society of polarised work–leisure relationships, or he will have a neutrality pattern of work and leisure and live in a society in which work and leisure are fairly self-contained.

The above explanations and suggestions are intended to show how philosophy (or 'world view'), society and individual are linked. If we are interested in the relationship between work and leisure at one of these levels, to understand it fully we must consider how it is reinforced or opposed at the other levels. To ask which is the better individual pattern of work and leisure is also to ask which is the better form of societal organisation of work and leisure and which, in this regard, is the more valid philosophy. To be able to make changes on any one of these levels we must concern ourselves with the implications that these changes may have for the other levels. Failure to do so will probably mean that no worthwhile change will be achieved.

9

The Microelectronics Revolution

Some observers of the recent rapid rate of technological change – which has been spearheaded but by no means confined to the development of the microprocessor or silicon 'chip' – believe that its economic and social consequences are so vast as to constitute a revolution. Others, while not denying that changes have taken place, question how far they have affected and will affect the fundamental nature of our society. The consequences of technological change fall into three broad groups: the effects on the nature, duration of and attitudes to work, the effects on leisure, and on the nature of the work–leisure relationship. We shall consider each of these topics in turn.

Effects on Work

The technology collectively referred to as microelectronics is the latest in a long line of applied inventions which have been changing the nature of industry and employment in industrial societies for at least two centuries. Microelectronics is the process of using microcircuits to reduce dramatically the cost of electronics and hence the cost of computing. The first computers, made only two or three decades ago, were large, costly and of limited application. With the introduction of silicon 'chips' (microcircuits containing many interconnected transistors) the electronic circuits of a small computer can be placed on one microprocessor or 'chip'. From being fast but blinkered workhorses, the latest computers have become dynamic, flexible information-processing systems capable of performing multitudes of different tasks (Evans, 1979).

The three main changes in computers resulting from microelectronics – big cost reduction, very small space and wide range of possible applicability – mean that the areas of use have increased and will increase greatly (Central Policy Review Staff, 1978). Some industries and some kinds of employment have been affected more than others. In so far as there is disagreement about the effect of microelectronics on employment, it is not about whether jobs will disappear

– which is generally conceded – but about how many and what kinds of job will disappear, and to what extent they will be replaced by employment generated elsewhere in the economy (Hull, 1980).

Estimates of the effects to date of microelectronics on employment and predictions about its future effects fall into two main groups: those looking at the total amount of employment and those more concerned with its distribution among different industries and types of occupation. The difference between these two approaches, however, is largely one of emphasis, since overall statements about employment are most sensibly based on an examination of its components. The predictions which have been made concerning the impact of micro-electronics on the economy and on employment cover the whole range, from economic expansion and job creation at one extreme to recession and large-scale persistent unemployment at the other (Thornton and Wheelock, 1980).

Extreme optimists are impressed by the array of new products based on microelectronic technology, many of them connected with the leisure industries and generating employment in manufacture, distribution and servicing: products such as electronic calculators, hi-fi equipment and television games. Thus Forte (1979) believes that 'microelectronics is currently creating more employment opportunities worldwide than redundancy in traditional industries'. The reference to 'worldwide' reminds us that industrial employment is being introduced into previously agrarian countries, while 'redundancy in traditional industries' is widespread in advanced industrial societies.

Another, more cautious form of optimism amounts to expressing a hope that what has not happened so far may happen in the future. For example, Dale and Williamson (1980) take the view that 'new jobs will come in the application and support of microprocessors in new and existing products, though how many jobs and in what industries we cannot say'. This sort of vague prediction stands a better chance of coming true than more precise forecasts, but it is hardly convincing.

There are also those who are pessimists, even alarmists, about the effect of microelectronics on employment. They emphasise what has already happened, that is, the rise in unemployment in the early 1980s in most advanced industrial societies, rather than what could happen in the future. They share with the optimists a recognition of trend and counter-trend, but differ about which is and will be the stronger. Thus Senker (1981) writes: 'Technological change and economic trends appear on balance to be exerting strong pressures to reduce employment opportunities . . . The prospects, especially in Britain, are alarming.'

There seems to be a reasonable amount of agreement about which types of industry and occupation are being and will be most affected by the spread of microelectronics. These include assembly work, repair and maintenance work and clerical work, in manufacturing industry but also in services such as banking and insurance (Barron and Curnow, 1979). With regard to one specific application of microelectronics, Dale and Williamson (1980) claim that robots are being used to replace human workers in highly repetitive, often unskilled tasks such as paint-spraying, routine assembly and welding car bodies. These jobs are not only tedious and mundane; they are often carried out in dirty, noisy and dangerous environments.

One can generalise, as does Martin (1978), that one of the promises held out by microelectronics is that all the boring jobs will be done by machines. However, it is also possible that what will result is an increasing polarisation between the technological elite and the relatively skill-less workforce. The latter, according to Marsh (1981), will do the boring jobs and the machines the interesting ones. This view is supported by the point that employers will only substitute a system for people if it pays them to do so (Jenkins and Sherman, 1981). Jobs such as those of cleaners, canteen workers and waiters, supermarket shelf stackers, all low paid and often done by women, will probably be relatively immune from technological replacement.

To understand the nature and consequences of recent technological changes it is necessary to put them into their historical perspective. The effect on jobs is severe in the short term and the effect on the employment structure and on work as an economic and social institution may be profound in the medium to long term, but the technology itself represents no sudden break with the past, rapid though its recent developments have been. As Stonier (1980) points out, the microprocessor does nothing radically different from its progenitor, the computer, but what it does it does faster, more reliably and more cheaply.

We are experiencing now the acceleration of a historical process which can be traced back at least two centuries, a process which involves a shift in the principal economic activities from manipulating land, through manipulating machines, to manipulating information. Over these two centuries the character of working life has changed dramatically and in the course of these changes many people have suffered, including those who have been unemployed for long periods. Automation, computers and now microtechnology may, in this perspective, be seen as a special case of the wider problem of mechanisation, which Encel (1980) shows to have a number of aspects, including:

(1) A continuous and accelerating process of specialisation, that is, the development, destruction and creation of jobs and occupations.

(2)   A high level of occupational mobility, so that the typical work-
      ing career is no longer that of doing the same job between 15 and
      65.
(3)   The systematic application of science and technology to produc-
      tion, distribution and organisation.
(4)   A steady decline in working hours for the mass of workers.
(5)   A steady rise in the level of formal education expected in a wide
      variety of jobs.
(6)   A large-scale shift from agriculture through manufacturing to
      service occupations, and in particular those concerned with the
      handling of information. (p. 22)

Above all, there is the growing problem of unemployment, not
unique to the present time, but novel in its occurrence in occupations
and industries previously scarcely affected by it. The new technology's main attribute seems to be its propensity to increase productivity rather than to stimulate the production of new goods and
services (Jenkins and Sherman, 1979). Employers will substitute technology for people if it pays them to do so and it is clear that microelectronics is making such substitution both feasible and profitable.
The job market is increasingly a buyer's market. At present the
general attitude of trade union leaders to the new technology has been
described as 'moderate and generally favourable', and Robins and
Webster (1982) quote a suggestion that union officials are not anxious
to appear to be Luddites. But, significantly, those authors add: 'Grass
roots feeling is another matter!'

Effects on Leisure

Our concern with the effects of technological change on leisure takes
two main forms. First, there is the way in which leisure activities have
changed and may be expected to change as a result of the application
of technology to those activities. Secondly, there is the question of
whether technology, being applied primarily in the sphere of industry
and employment, will enable more creative forms of leisure to be
revived or introduced. These concerns may be summarised respectively as 'technological leisure' and 'the creative use of leisure'.

In-home leisure in this future age of technological wonders extends
far beyond what is available today. Not only will 'telesensing' be
wall-sized, offer a fantastic store of programs through its interactive
cable system, and instantaneously reproduce any event around the
world; but it will have sound and sensual capabilities to provide a
total experience far richer than the cool little visual screen of primi-

tive television ... Electronics will also offer whole libraries of literature and music, a variety of interactive games, and instantaneous visual communication throughout the affluent world. The mushrooming growth of destination leisure in the later twentieth century barely gave a hint of the future ... it will be possible to be on almost any island, coast or resort area in a few hours and go from city to city in supersonic minutes ... A vast spectrum of leisure goods will be available through commercial and public provisions to enable a person to select stimuli, entertainment, food and drink, cultural enrichment, and physical challenge with a speed and convenience that makes the home a leisure center and every community a full-service resort.

These are extracts from 'The future of leisure: a scenario', by Kelly (1982, p. 277). The picture painted is part fact and part speculation based on an extrapolation of present trends. Kelly does not explicitly invite his readers to ponder whether they like the idea of such a future, nor does he offer his own opinion about its desirability. His 'scenario' is significant because much of it has already come to pass or is known to be technically possible within the next few years. The transistor has already made possible a range of games, communication devices and entertainments unimagined a few years ago. Other technologies have made travel to leisure destinations faster and less expensive, and television has both introduced more people to leisure activities and experiences new to them and created mass audiences for activities, such as snooker and darts, previously with only minority audiences or none at all.

For some years now, computers have featured in the organisation and experience of various leisure activities. They have been used for score-keeping, judging, and for analysing play in different sports (Teague and Erickson, 1974). They have made simulation possible, for example, with indoor golf driving ranges, and have enabled animated films to be prepared and music composed. Microelectronics have extended these applications (for example, computer-based chess) although it is fair to characterise them as mainly 'games, gambling and a variety of standardised amusements' (Laver, 1980).

It is relatively simple to document the ways in which technology has influenced what might be called the paraphernalia of leisure. It is more difficult to assess the qualitative effects (if any) and to evaluate the extent to which leisure has become more creative or less creative as a result of the application of technology. Not all of the attempts to portray the leisure of the future do so in Kelly's somewhat mechanistic terms. Some – who may be called the cultural optimists – believe that the release of the majority of the population from the necessity to be employed will enable at least some of them to become more creative than now. Thus while Martin (1978) extrapolates present trends in seeing many people 'sitting in front of their wall screens with a carton of beer', he also predicts that 'a small proportion of the future leisured class will probably be far more creative than they could possibly have been with a full-time job'. He draws a parallel between the wealthy and non-employed class in Victorian England, many of whom were inventors, writers, amateur scientists, musicians, and so on, and the potentialities of the future non-employed. But the creative Victorians were a minority and were well-educated. Tomorrow's non-employed threaten to be a much larger minority, perhaps even a majority, and their level of education (given present trends) must be in doubt.

Many years ago Bernal (1939) saw the effects of technology on leisure as productive of both actual passivity and potential creativity:

> The new techniques of cinema, wireless and television have other possibilities than providing fantasy escape from life ... [they] are a means for enormously increasing the range of human experience ... Creative leisure, too, can be developed through science ... Science itself may become for many an absorbing recreation. (pp. 358–9)

Things have not changed all that much in the intervening years. Technology as applied to leisure is more sophisticated – but not noticeably more likely to enhance sociability or personal development. Today's electronic games and video equipment have been castigated as producing an anaesthetising effect in opposition to the notions of autonomy and power which some see as central to the definition of leisure (Coalter, 1982).

Despite the evidence that technology applied to leisure has so far led more to passivity than to creativity, the hope remains that things will change in the future. This hope is based on the assumption that technology will increasingly reduce the amount of time that each of us has to spend in employment producing the goods and services that we need and that more time will be freed for leisure, including leisure spent 'working' on activities of our own choice. This leads us to consider the influence of technology, not just on work and leisure separately, but on the relationship between the two.

Effects on the Work–Leisure Relationship

A number of propositions have been put forward concerning the ways in which advancing technology is changing and will change the nature of the relationship between work and leisure. These propositions may be summarised as:

(1) Leisure will take on more of the character of work.
(2) There will be less distinction between work and leisure.
(3) Attitudes and values will change.
(4) Individual differences will increasingly be recognised.

Technology, in opening up the possibility of less time in employment, also encourages the suggestion that some of the increased leisure time could be used for work of our own choice. Since most of us have been accustomed to spending a substantial proportion of our time and energies 'at work', it is argued that increased leisure time cannot entirely be filled by rest and relaxation or by passive consumption of entertainment. As Brutzkus (1980) puts it, 'if the mental balance of people is not to become distorted they must find an "activated" leisure'. This means that some 'leisure' time would become purposeful and constitute what might be called a 'second economy' beyond the basic economy producing goods and services on a large scale. The basic economy would be primarily concerned with productivity and output, the second economy with the significance of work for human life and civilisation. Activities in the second economy would include small-scale agriculture and handicrafts, artistic and cultural pursuits, political activities and public service of various kinds.

Another way in which technology may result in leisure taking on more of the character of work is that the basic economy may be more permeated by leisure values. This assumes that the new technology can just as well be used to create satisfying jobs and enhance human skills as to destroy and debase jobs (Council for Science and Society, 1981). It is claimed that many people, given the choice, would probably prefer to take some part of the benefits of increased productivity in the form of better-quality goods of more individual design, better housing and improved social services such as education and health care, rather than accept all of the benefit in increased leisure. It is difficult to determine how far this claim is true, since this sort of choice cannot be made at the individual level but must depend on political decisions influenced by effective pressure groups and public opinion.

The second proposition is that technology will increasingly bring about a blurring of the distinction between work and leisure. This is related to the first proposition, but instead of a 'second economy' of leisure the prediction is that the one economy will be revolutionised to integrate work and leisure values. Toffler (1980) expresses one mode of this process in his concept of 'prosuming': the act of producing goods and services for our own use. The integration of work and leisure, however, is only partial – there is still a 'sector B' of the economy in which paid work is done for a minimum time and with maximum use of technology. It is 'sector A' in which 'self-directed and self-monitored work' is to take place and which has some of the characteristics of leisure. This is also the idea behind Gershuny's (1978) concept of the emerging self-service economy: more work to be done in the home, making, for example, furniture or crockery, instead of routinised employment outside the home. New information technology is improving communications to the extent that, for increasing numbers of people, home can become workplace.

A third approach invites us to consider how attitudes and values relating to work and leisure may change as a result of technological developments. The work ethic which has been strong for the last two centuries, but now shows signs of weakening, places work at the centre of the meaning and purpose of life with leisure as its servant. A leisure ethic would seek to reverse these priorities and make leisure the central area of meaning, fulfilment and personal identity, with work as a means to these ends. Perceptive critics of the work ethic, however, do not want to abolish work – rather, they want to retain and enhance its creative functions while imbuing it with qualities such as choice and pleasurable activity which are now often associated only with leisure.

Among those who think along these lines, Jenkins and Sherman (1981) have proposed a 'usefulness' ethic to replace the work ethic. They see technology as producing 'the collapse of work' (or, more precisely, the reduction of employment) but they believe that

> many people feel guilty if they spend their time enjoying themselves rather than doing things; many people are so attached to work that they will need to be weaned off it. Doing things, either for other people or for yourself or family, implies that the time is not wasted. In a great many respects a lot of constructive leisure activities could be what is currently described as work. (p. 85)

But a 'usefulness' ethic still has a strong flavour of work – perhaps it would be better to regard such an ethic as an intermediate stage on the way to a fuller integration of work and leisure.

Another critic both of the social consequences of technology and of the leisure ethic as replacing the work ethic sees as the culprit the notion that machines should save labour:

> We have convinced millions of toiling men and women that work ideally belongs to machines, that progress means 'saving' labour by relinquishing it to machines, which will always do it better. So they begin to see leisure, not work, as the proper arena of creativity, freedom, growth. They dream that perhaps one day soon, when

progress is complete, we shall all live in a workless world . . . where work once stood at the center of life as an indispensable aspect of responsible adulthood, we have instead recreation . . . play . . . hobbies . . . the joy of sex . . . fun and games, all of which finally seem to come down to a sort of full-time, gourmet consumerism: cultivating extravagant wants, buying things, using them up, buying more. (Roszak, 1979, p. 231)

Roszak argues that, rather than save labour, we should aim to preserve it from indiscriminate technological advance. Like Jenkins and Sherman, he expresses reservations (on other people's behalf) about their ability to cope with leisure. But his picture of current leisure consumerism is well drawn and is reminiscent of Godbey's (1975) concept of anti-leisure: the work-obsessed approach to leisure activities and experiences. Technology's direct contribution to work–leisure integration is probably small. It may be, as Mesthene (1969) suggests, that the way technological change produces value change is by opening up new options for choice. In making goods and services easier to produce, it may lead us to question how far we want work and leisure values to feature in the use of our time and the meaning of our activities.

The fourth proposition concerning technology's influence on the work–leisure relationship is that it can lead to greater recognition of individual differences in the need for work and leisure activities and experiences. There are really two propositions here: one is that men and women can be shown to vary in their present needs for work and leisure (hence generalisations are dangerous) and the other concerns the extent to which people can change their perceptions of, and hence their 'needs' for, work and leisure.

Time freed from employment has already increased to a point where we can see how some people have reacted to this freedom. For example, some have found early retirement pleasurable and rewarding while others have not, depending to a large extent on whether they have financial and inner resources to cope with it (Parker, 1982). We have been socialised to believe that work is good and idleness is bad, and the proposition that 'people feel guilty if they are not working hard' has been wrongly elevated to a truth about human nature. As noted in Chapter 2, some members of primitive societies are content to be idle, to have the freedom to do nothing very active at all. Though they have work to do from time to time, they are not bored by the absence of work or of the kind of games we invent to compensate for its absence. Perhaps, as Rothman and Mossman (1972) suggest, the inability to cope with leisure is only a passing phenomenon of our highly industrialised society.

10

The Potentialities of Work and Leisure

In these final two chapters my main concern will be to see how the type of philosophy and social structure affect individual work–leisure relationships, both as they are and as they could be. This chapter will consider first the possibility that there exist broad types of person with respect to seeking fulfilment in either work or leisure. Then the way in which work and leisure spheres confront each other in contemporary industrial society will be posed as a problem, and it will be suggested there are two main kinds of answer: the *differentiation* or the *integration* of work and leisure. Finally, these alternatives will be discussed in the light of their potentialities to fulfil human needs.

Types of Person

Studies of different work situations and of individual involvement in work clearly show the wide variation in content and conditions of work in modern industrial societies and the range of involvement from almost complete identification to almost complete estrangement or alienation. There arises the question of the extent to which there exist different types of person with respect to the needs which are satisfied mainly in work or in leisure, as well as in different types of work situation and work involvement. This question is asked mainly by psychologists, whose special interest is individual behaviour, but it also has relevance for sociologists, whose special interests include socially patterned behaviour. We may approach this problem by quoting the views of a psychologist (Fraser, 1962) who is concerned with the philosophical question of the meaning that work ought to have in a person's life:

Ought [the individual] to find in [work] his principal means of self-expression? Ought it to be the cause of his deepest satisfactions? Should it be the biggest thing in his life? This is to demand a great deal both of the individual and the job, and it is unlikely that more than a small proportion of any community will ever approach such a standard. Nor may it be desirable that they should, for the number of individuals who have this level of motivation to pour into their work is limited, while the number of jobs into which it would be worth pouring it is similarly restricted. On the other hand, ought work to make as few demands as possible on the individual? Ought it to offer only a limited sense of achievement or identification? Ought it to become a means of putting in part of the day quite agreeably while at the same time providing the where-withal to finance his home and leisure pursuits? There are indivi-duals to whom a job like this would make a strong appeal and who might find their real satisfactions in other areas of their life. Between these extremes there will be jobs and individuals with different levels of expectation and satisfaction to offer and receive, and if we were to match up each with the other we might claim to have achieved the ideal industrial community. Those who expected a great deal from their work and were prepared to put a lot into it would be in jobs which utilized all their potentialities to the full and gave them in return a deep sense of personal achievement. Those who neither expected nor were prepared to contribute very much would be in the comfortable, undemanding jobs where they would be reasonably occupied, well paid and contented. (pp. 176–7)

There is a curious mixture of narrowness and breadth of vision in Fraser's remarks. He raises the prescriptive question of the place of work in human life and at the beginning appears to be discussing the potentialities of man in general rather than of men and women of a particular time and place. Yet his statements about the proportion of men with high work motivation and 'the number of jobs into which it would be worth pouring it' are largely descriptive. He appears to be treating the level of work motivation as something which is entirely a personal characteristic of individuals, independent of the kind of work which may be open to them and unaffected by their experience of work which has the potentiality for changing the attitudes of those who do it. It is true that, by the standards of those whose work has reasonable scope for personal involvement, there are relatively few jobs today which reach these standards. However, there is nothing immutable about the proportion of jobs which people may regard as worthy of personal involvement. The criteria of estimation of worth may change, but so may the content and conditions of the jobs. Whether the latter happens or not is largely a matter of whether enough people agitate for changes which would make their work a more rewarding personal experience.

The idea of matching levels of personal work involvement to levels of objectively 'involving' work is superficially attractive, but assumes both personal attitudes and occupational structures to be constants. It is true that we know very little about the relative contributions of initial personal preferences and subsequent work experiences in shaping present work and leisure values. It is very difficult, for example, to say to what extent social workers tend to be highly work-involved and therefore need less leisure because of the nature of the work they do or because, being the sort of people they are, they were led to seek highly demanding work. But we certainly should not ignore the feedback effect that work experiences can have on changing people's initial values and motivations. There was evidence of this in the pilot interviews with older informants in business and service occupations; a few of them could recall their early feelings about the work they entered and how different these were from the pattern of adjustment to circumstances which they had subsequently worked out. Thus one insurance manager, having started out in the business world many years ago with a good education and high hopes, somewhat sadly remarked that 'your abilities and potentialities tend to equate themselves with the work you do'.

If we were to adopt the 'matching' idea suggested by Fraser we should need to be quite clear about what we were matching with what. Presumably the matching would not be done until after school-leaving age. But already certain differences in attitude to work would have emerged which could not be attributed wholly to differences in personality type. Assuming the present structure of family life and education, some children would have been brought up in a home and school environment that would encourage them to seek interest and a sense of achievement from work, while others would expect little from work and therefore feel 'satisfied' with low-level occupations. The occupational structure, too, would be regarded as given. Jobs which presumably would be regarded as unsuitable for those with high work involvement would be offered to those who 'neither expected nor were prepared to contribute very much', as a result of which the latter would never know how much they might be prepared to contribute if they were placed in a work environment that encouraged contribution.

To adapt a Marxist phrase used in connection with society as a whole to the sphere of work and leisure, it scarcely seems an exaggeration to say that there are 'two classes in society': the privileged with respect to a unified and fulfilling work–leisure life, and the underprivileged. As Durant (1938) remarked, for some men and women the problem of leisure does not arise:

> They all obtain satisfaction from their work. All of them have some sphere of independent action, or they are presented with problems

and difficulties with which they must grapple and solve; none of them are automata ... Because of this, and because, finding satisfaction in their work, they do not desire to flee from it as soon as the immediate job is completed, the impact of their profession or work is clearly discernible in all their activities. There is for them no sharp break. They read books which have relevance to their job; similarly they attend lectures and follow courses of study; they move predominantly amongst people who have the same interests ... In short, the method of earning their livelihood determines for them their mode of living. And it does this in such a way that they obtain satisfaction. Hence they need not search for compensations in other directions; they do not require soporifics from the world of amusement ... they will tend to bring to such aspects of their lives the same attitude and qualities of mind as are required and developed by their work. (p. 250)

My research confirms that there is a group of people who tend to have such a work–leisure pattern, and that there are two other groups who differ from it but who for the present purpose may be considered as one. So far my major concern has been to establish that certain associations between work and leisure variables exist, without necessarily implying a causal relationship. My view is that the causal influence is more likely to be *from* work experiences and attitudes *to* leisure experiences and attitudes than the other way round, mainly because the work sphere is both more structured and more basic to life itself, although I also believe that there is something to say for Burns's (1967) proposition that there 'is a tendency for the organising principles of leisure to extend into work life'. But which is cause and which is effect is not crucial to the description of the quality of the relationship. In terms of individuals, the point is that some men and women in the past have led, and some today do lead 'unitary lives in which the excellence obtainable during leisure characterizes the work in which they engage' (Weiss, 1960), while others – the underprivileged – have 'excellence' in neither sphere. The question then arises: to what extent is this distribution of excellence the inevitable product of personality differences rooted in human nature, or the potentially changeable product of a particular type of social structure which distributes the 'means to excellence' unevenly?

A full answer to this question would require research beyond any that has so far been carried out. Ideally it would require a long-term research project so that certain types of personality could be identified before they entered the world of work and could then be followed up to see to what extent their subsequent work and leisure behaviour and attitudes corresponded to a predicted pattern. In the absence of such

research, we should keep an open mind about the relative effects of
'nature' and 'nurture' in this respect.

Problem: the Confrontation of Work and Leisure

The quality of the work and leisure lives of the mass of people in a
society becomes a problem when the confrontation of the two spheres
reveals shortcomings in either or both, or when a minority appears to
have achieved conditions and satisfactions which give the majority a
sense of relative deprivation. The view that there are two kinds of
person with respect to the seeking of fulfilment in either work or
leisure does not avoid the perception of a problem, but defines its
terms fairly narrowly: how to adjust kinds of person to kinds of
potentially fulfilling situations within something like the present division of labour and leisure. But if we reject the view that there are two
such kinds of person the problem becomes much wider: what kind of
social structure is necessary to give *all* people opportunities for fulfilment in work *and* leisure, and how can various individual needs be
reconciled with the 'needs' of society itself? To implement this could
involve a radically new division of labour and leisure. Before considering the policy aspects of these questions, it may be helpful to seek
to clarify the ways in which the confrontation of work and leisure
poses problems for contemporary industrial society, and the possible
ways in which these problems may be resolved.

In pre-industrial societies there was no confrontation between
work and leisure because work itself contained such leisure-like activities as society could afford its members. At the height of the
Industrial Revolution work (which had been purged of much of its
leisure content by the Protestant work ethic for the middle classes
and by factory work subsistence wage levels for the working class)
confronted a leisure scarcely worth the name. It is only in the
modern phase of industrialism, with the shorter working week and
greater purchasing power of the masses, that leisure has become a
separate and significant part of life. But, as we have shown, there are
the privileged and the underprivileged with respect to rewarding
work and leisure experiences. Assuming that these differences cannot
be explained wholly in terms of differences in personality type, there
is the question of what to do about the underprivileged. To put the
problem simply: a large number of men and women today have
work and leisure lives which are neither satisfying nor creative. What
should be done?

A number of detailed answers are possible, but they may be
grouped into two general types: those which stem from the two
philosophies of segmentalism and holism. The guiding principles of

these answers are, respectively, differentiation and integration and they will be considered in turn.

Answer 1: the Differentiation of Work and Leisure

Those who advocate the differentiation of work and leisure as the solution to at least some of the problems in either sphere do so on the assumption, explicit or implicit, that the segmentation of spheres is a characteristic and desirable feature of modern industrial society. Dubin (1963) puts this point of view as follows:

> I assume that modern urban-industrial life is highly segmented, and that at a behavioural level this is its very central feature. All of what we mean by secularization of life, by freedom, and by privacy derives from this segmented and compartmented way in which modern life is lived out. Indeed, I would be constrained to argue that the rate of innovation and the radicalness of innovations in all realms of modern living (from the arts, through science and technology, through social relations tó morals and values) can be traced directly to the segmentation of the realms of life. I would go further and argue that the adjustment of individual to society is enhanced on a probabilistic basis, for there are now manifestly more niches into which any individual can 'fit' and among which he may choose insofar as personal choice is a factor in finding a place in the modern community.

There are two distinct ideas in what Dubin is saying here: the understanding that society is segmented and the belief that the perceived segmentation encourages innovation and the adjustment of individuals to society. As applied to work and leisure, the first proposition relates to the 'polarity' hypothesis, evidence for and against which was reviewed in Chapter 7. Here we are mainly concerned with the second proposition in that it relates to the realisation of social and individual potentialities.

There can be little quarrel with that part of the proposition concerning innovation in all realms of modern life. Segmentation (including differentiation of structure and function and manifest in such features as the division of labour and complex organisations) is unquestionably a characteristic of the development of modern society. The controversial issue concerns the adjustment of the individual to society. The model of society implicit in the statement that 'there are now manifestly many more niches into which any given individual can "fit"' is one in which such fitting or not fitting is the result of a transaction between the individual and society. It is the task of society, this argument runs, not to impose a pattern of social relationships on the individual but to offer him a set of alternatives. Dubin is in effect arguing that a society in which failure to 'adjust' in one sphere means failure to 'adjust' in all spheres is less desirable than a society in which failure is compartmentalised and therefore restricted. Most people would agree that it is better to have a choice of opportunities to adjust than a compulsion to adjust to a totalitarian society. But we must not imagine that the life spheres of individuals and the institutions of modern industrial societies are more autonomous than they actually are. It may sound a superficially attractive solution to say 'if our work doesn't offer us a chance to think and be creative we must compensate for this in leisure'. However, there must be considerable doubt about the quality of the 'success' obtainable in one isolated sphere.

Friedmann (1961) is one of the best-known exponents of the doctrine of the differentiation of work and leisure as the answer to problems in both spheres. He does not in the long run abandon the task of 'humanising' work, as some others do, and so his views represent the case for differentiation in perhaps its strongest form

> First, there must be a revaluation of work, which, to be complete, must be carried out simultaneously on three different planes, intellectual, social and moral. Secondly, there must be opportunities for self-realization and self-development for the individual in non-work activities. (p. 152)

He sees greater progress being made towards the latter goal, since 'there are still today millions of jobs which cannot be revalued in such ways, and this will continue to be the case for a long while yet'. His pessimism about the possibility of work revaluation makes him write, in connection with the reduction of working hours resulting from automation, of 'the need to find a new centre for human development in the hours thus freed, i.e. in the active use of leisure'.

The trouble with Friedmann's views is that they appear to be advocating changes in both work and leisure spheres but in fact the key to the whole problem is seen as leisure. Making leisure 'a new centre' is something we can do fairly easily, he implies, while the reorganisation of work is much more difficult. Two things have to be done, the one short-term and relatively easy to accomplish, the other long-term and much more difficult. Let us, he argues, tackle the easier part of the programme first. Unfortunately, this approach usually means that the more difficult part of the programme is deferred indefinitely. Moreover, the victories that are gained in one field are nullified if the campaign is never started in the other. From time to time people who have been deprived in both their work and leisure lives are given the opportunity, through a large football pools win, to make leisure the centre of their lives. On the whole they do not make a success of this and there is no reason to suppose that a society that seeks to make leisure the 'centre for human development', while leaving the problem of work untackled, will succeed any better.

Another French writer, Ellul (1965), challenges Friedmann's views:

Friedmann writes 'We must conjure up the prospect of a society in which labour will be of restricted duration, industrial operations automatized, and piecework, requiring no attention, made pleasant by music and lectures ... a society, in short, in which culture will be identified completely with leisure. In a leisure more and more full of potentialities, and more and more active, will be found the justification of the humanistic experiment.'

Friedmann is asserting here that it is impossible to make indust-rial labour positive. But if we agree to Friedmann's proposition that the human being can develop his personality only in the cultivation of leisure, we are denying that work is an element of personality fulfilment, or of satisfaction, or of happiness. This is bad enough; but the situation is even more serious when we consider that put-ting our hopes in leisure is really taking refuge in idealism. If leisure were a real vacuum, a break with the forces of the environment, and if, moreover, it were spontaneously utilized for the education of the personality, the thesis of the value of leisure might hold. But neither of these conditions is true.

We see first of all that leisure, instead of being a vacuum repre-senting a break with society, is literally stuffed with technical mechanisms of compensation and integration ... Leisure time is a mechanized time and is exploited by techniques which, although different from those of man's ordinary work, are as invasive, exact-ing, and leave man no more free than labour itself. As to the second condition, it is simply not the case that the individual, left on his own, will devote himself to the education of his personality or to a spiritual and cultural life ... We conclude that the education of the human personality cannot but conform to the postulates of techni-cal civilization. Man's leisure must reinforce the other elements of this culture so that there will be no risk of producing poorly adjusted persons. This is the direction the techniques of amusement have taken. To gamble that leisure will enable man to live is to sanction the dissociation I have been describing and to cut him off completely from a part of life. (pp. 400–2)

Ellul's language is impassioned, but what he says is more in line with such facts as we have about the relationship between work and leisure than the apparently more practical, but in fact more idealistic, position of Friedmann. The confrontation of Friedmann's views by those of Ellul may be compared with the change in the views of David Riesman (1958) over a period:

> my collaborators and I in *The Lonely Crowd* took it for granted that it was impossible to reverse the trend towards automation; we assumed that the current efforts to make work more meaningful – which by and large succeeded only in making it more time-consuming and gregarious but not more challenging – might as well be given up, with the meaning of life to be sought henceforth in the creative use of leisure.

But Riesman's subsequent consideration of research findings led him to the view that

> it might be easier to make leisure more meaningful if one at the same time could make work more demanding ... It may be slightly less difficult to reorganize work routines so that they become less routine, more challenging, and hence more instructive, than to cope all at once with the burdens placed on leisure by the evaporation of the meaning of work ... I believe that we cannot take advantage of what remains of our pre-industrial heritage to make leisure more creative, individually and socially, if work is not creative, too.

The solutions put forward by Friedmann and in the early work of Riesman, while based on the differentiation of work and leisure, involve only a certain degree of pessimism about 'humanising' the former and not a desire to write it off altogether as a source of human fulfilment. A few writers, however, have suggested just that. Fairchild is quoted as saying:

> Work must be recognized not as a virtue or a blessing, but as an intrinsic evil. The only justification for work is its product ... We must come to realize that leisure time, that is, time spent in pleasurable employment, is the only kind of time that makes life worth living. (in Barnes and Ruedi, 1950, p. 810)

Marcuse (1962) looks forward to society being organised 'with a view to saving time and space for the development of individuality *outside* the inevitably repressive work-world'. A less extreme view, but one still dismissive of work, is held by Vincent and Mayers (1959): 'Man faces the prospect of making work shorter and less onerous, of combining it with play, and then of making play primary and work secondary.' In answering Friedmann, Ellul has also implicitly answered these writers.

We may now turn to the second general answer to the problem of the confrontation of work and leisure.

Answer 2: the Integration of Work and Leisure

In previous chapters evidence was given that work is not a central life interest for most manual and the business type of non-manual employees. But the division of life into spheres which can be ranked in order of providing centrality of interest or satisfaction is somewhat artificial. In line with the Japanese workers quoted earlier who favoured an ideal pattern of integrated work and leisure, a number of both manual and non-manual informants in my surveys answered the question about ambition in life in terms which spanned both work and non-work spheres: for example, 'to make my life a success' or 'to create a position where my occupation and private life are running as one'. Also, it may be somewhat misleading to speak of 'integration' as if it applied only to spheres of life: for some men – and particularly women – integration is more a matter of self-realisation through relationships with others, cutting across work and non-work spheres.

Friedlander (1966) is one of the few writers who have discussed the integration of work and leisure on the basis of his own research. In the concluding remarks to his study of manual and non-manual government employees he states that 'one may well question the extent to which recreation will prove an even partial substitute for work as an opportunity for meaningful environmental interaction'. If that is true of recreation, it is probably just as true of the other functions of leisure. Personal development is hardly likely to be enhanced by a withdrawal from the more rewarding kind of work, since, as Wilensky (1964) points out, 'among men not accustomed to the wider universe made available by demanding work, it takes a long, expensive education to avoid an impoverished life'.

Hollander (1966) expresses the aim of integration thus:

> the long-range goal is not only to maximize leisure time but also to fuse it with a uniquely satisfying form of work. Indeed, the projected fusion of work with creativity lends a totally new complexion to the whole concept of leisure, making it more difficult to differentiate it from this new kind of work. (p. 179)

In this fusion, work may lose its present characteristic feature of constraint and gain the creativity now associated mainly with leisure, while leisure may lose its present characteristic feature of opposition to work and gain the status – now associated mainly with the *product* of work – of a resource worthy of planning and developing to provide the greatest possible human satisfaction.

Those who propose an integration of work and leisure disagree with the advocates of differentiation not only in their proposed solution to the problem but also in their perception of the present state of affairs. Whereas the segmentalists see work and leisure as compartments of life and society, the holists see a relationship between present work and leisure, though not yet an organic one. According to Seligman (1965),

leisure becomes a social problem when its purpose, the regeneration of the human being, is denied or debased. Regeneration can be realized only when leisure confronts work which is meaningful. Then the human spirit recoups its energies for another bout with nature. In a sense leisure is earned through such a confrontation. But under modern technology free time can be used only as an escape from the oppressiveness of the industrial system. However ... free time is itself 'industrialized'; hence there is no genuine escape. Moreover, under automation, leisure's task is to fill empty time, something that modern man does poorly anyway. The irony is that work is employed to supply leisure with objects to make the latter ostensibly enjoyable, while leisure is frequently used to advance one's status in work as on the golf course, or in the upper reaches of the corporate milieu. But there is no organic relationship here: all that is visible is a mechanistic exploitation of one realm by the other. Besides, the use of leisure as a leverage in work is reserved to the upper classes in our society. (p. 354)

It might be added that leisure is 'frequently used to advance one's status in work' only by those who are imbued with the Protestant work ethic and who do not know how to enjoy leisure for its own sake. But the point about mechanistic exploitation of one realm by the other is well taken − whether it is Aristotle's 'we labour in order to have leisure' or the industrial recreationist's 'we have leisure in order to labour better'. In individual psychological terms, too, integration of spheres may be a more stable situation and easier to maintain than a split consciousness. Keniston (1962) writes:

The man who spends his working day at a job whose primary meaning is merely to earn enough money to enable him to enjoy the rest of his time can seldom really enjoy his leisure, his family, or his avocations. Life is of a piece, and if work is empty or routine, the rest will inevitably become contaminated as well, becoming a compulsive escape or a driven effort to compensate for the absent satisfactions that should inhere in work. Similarly, to try to avoid social and political problems by cultivating one's garden can at best be only partly successful. When the effects of government and society are so ubiquitous, one can escape them only in the back-waters, and then only for a short while. Putting work, society and politics into one pigeonhole, and family, leisure and enjoyment into another creates a compartmentalization which is in continual danger of collapsing. Or, put more precisely, such a division of life into nonoverlapping spheres merely creates a new psychological strain, the almost impossible strain of artificially maintaining a continually split outlook. (p. 145)

The case in favour of an integration of work and leisure turns out to be mainly a critique of what various forms of differentiation have failed to achieve. This is perhaps unavoidable at the present stage of social development. We have no set of social institutions and corres-ponding cultural patterns which represent in daily life an integration of work and leisure – we have, at most, the behaviour and attitudes of a comparatively few individuals sharing certain patterns of living which indicate what that integration could be. Even this kind of guide may be misleading, for change at the societal level is not, for example, a matter of seeking to extend the life patterns of residential social workers to embrace all kinds of workers. It is much more flexible and multifaceted than that.

The wider realisation of human potentialities is clearly a long-term goal, although this does not mean that we cannot take short-term steps in that direction. To reconcile work with leisure, to show how the one can enhance the other, may take some time, for we have long thought of work as the opposite of leisure. Making efforts here and there to ameliorate working conditions or to enhance the experience of leisure are valuable activities, but they may do no more than help us to hold our own against the sweeping tide of technological and mar-keting society. A sociological imagination that reminds us of the real range of social behaviour is necessary so that we can collectively decide which kinds of work and which kinds of leisure are appropriate to a good life and create the opportunities for these to be realised.

11

Social Policies in the 1980s and 1990s

Finally we come to consider the implications of what has been said in previous chapters for social policies dealing with problems of work and leisure. We shall first assess two alternative types of general policy based on contrasting social theories – segmentalist and holist. The possibility of revaluing work and leisure as spheres of life will then be discussed, followed by an assessment of some of the scenarios that have been put forward. We shall examine the key role of education in all these possible changes and, to conclude, some practical problems in planning for work and leisure will be reviewed.

Segmentalist Policies

It is possible to examine the segmentalist proposals for work and leisure in relative isolation from each other, although it may be useful to distinguish the 'neutrality' from the 'opposition' approach. As a starting point we may consider the three 'solutions to the problem of stultifying labour' outlined by Wilensky (1960), to

> (1) develop patterns of creative, challenging leisure to compensate for an inevitable spread in dehumanized labour; (2) offer vastly better compensation for those condemned to alienating work situations (the trade union solution of more money for less working-time . . . ; (3) redesign the workplace and the technology to invest work with more meaning, and hence enhance the quality of leisure. (p. 546)

These three proposed solutions may be related respectively to the three patterns of work–leisure relationship: neutrality, opposition (both involving a segmentalist view of society) and extension (involving a holist view of society). Although the first solution includes the word 'compensation' and to that extent implies a recognition of some kind of relationship between work and leisure, it suggests that 'de-humanized' labour can be tolerated if it is kept separate from a creative, challenging leisure. As we have seen, there must be grave doubts about how far this can be achieved. Attempts to do so, however, appeal to those who despair of making drastic changes in the work content and conditions of the mass of people, at least in the short run. The industrial recreation movement, the government and local authority sponsored sports and recreation facilities are examples of this kind of solution.

The second proposed solution is a more straightforward acceptance that leisure is the opposite of work. Although Wilensky may not have intended to differentiate between 'dehumanized labour' in the first solution and 'alienating work situations' in the second, it may nevertheless be useful to draw some such distinction. The crucial difference appears to lie in the nature of the compensation offered. In the first case it is entirely in non-work terms: in return for acceptance of a whole package of 'dehumanized labour', a more attractive leisure package is offered. In the second case the compensation is both within and outside the work sphere: although the work situation itself is not altered, the hours of work may be shortened or the economic rewards increased. The difference between the two solutions may be expressed as society making two compensatory propositions to those whose work it recognises to be intrinsically unpleasant or unsatisfying: (1) 'We know it's boring, but put up with it and we shall make it up to you in leisure', or (2) 'We know it's damaging, but you need only do it for a short time and we shall pay you well for it'.

It seems likely that boring and uncreative work will be with us for longer than damaging work. Work which leaves no obvious mark on the body or the life of the employee is less likely to attract widespread criticism and demands for reform than work which is self-evidently harmful. The number of 'extreme' occupations (extreme in the sense of danger or physical strain) is diminishing. Wherever possible, machines are used to do such work, not necessarily from any humanitarian motives (though, as with the abolition of slavery, these no doubt play a part) but because it is usually more economically advantageous to do so. Also, the role of the trade unions in campaigning for greater regard to be paid to health and safety in industry must not be overlooked. However, much less concern is expressed about work which is relatively safe and harmless to physical health but which has a low potential for human satisfaction and feelings of creativity. The role of the time-study man, which is essentially that of a technician looking upon man as a mere tool to be 'serviced' so that he can work as rapidly and effectively as possible, is generally accepted. It is left to industrial psychologists and sociologists to insist that man has a fundamental need to participate in the work he does and to recommend that it should be organised in ways that would develop his personality and make it a meaningful experience and not just a time-passing routine.

The reasons for the greater popularity of segmentalist solutions to problems of work are not hard to find. They have the obvious merit of being applicable on a small scale and do not require the amount of research and education of public opinion that would be entailed in more holist solutions. Segmentalist solutions aim at limited goals which are therefore more easily achieved, and their programmes tend to flow from obvious rather than imaginative comparisons. Thus the goal that workers usually set themselves (or that is set for them by their representatives) is to obtain the best possible income and working conditions which any comparable group of workers has achieved. The 'differentials' are the subject of much concern, but they are actual differentials between groups of workers – not the differential between existing and potential conditions given a possible restructuring of society and its values.

The segmentalist approach to leisure is parallel to the approach to work. Since the influence on leisure of other spheres of life is discounted, attempts are made to change it as a more or less self-contained sphere. The aim to 'develop patterns of creative, challenging leisure' does not depend on the individual bringing to it values and experiences gained in other spheres of life, and so the question of how these new patterns of leisure are to be developed becomes important. In a society in which the provision of leisure goods and services has become a major industry there is no great problem of access to the means of spending leisure time, assuming that one has also money to spend. For the segmentalist, a greater problem may be how to encourage people to spend their leisure time in ways which are socially acceptable, because segmentalism rarely extends to a complete unconcern with the effects on society of 'undesirable' activities.

In Britain there is considerable concern about the ways in which certain groups – especially the more rebellious types of young people – spend their leisure time. The Youth Service, religious and other welfare organisations are doing something to provide leisure facilities for young people. The Sports Council has taken a number of initiatives in promoting sporting activities among this age-group, especially the unemployed and those living in deprived areas – for example, a sports leadership programme in three areas of London (Sheridan, 1982). But such campaigns have been criticised as dealing with symptoms rather than causes and as failing to understand the multiple deprivations from which many working-class youngsters suffer (Corrigan, 1982).

In America a movement has been developing which has so far hardly started in Britain but which clearly has potentialities for crossing the Atlantic. That movement is professional recreation, and its personnel, paid and voluntary, are variously known as professional recreation workers, recreationists, leisurists and even recreators. The main assumptions and aims of this movement have been put frankly by Sutherland (1957): 'Since the average citizen is unable to invent new uses for his leisure, a professional elite shares a heavy responsibility for discovering criteria for ways of employing leisure and creating enthusiasms for common ends within the moral aims of the community.' The key phrases in this statement are 'professional elite' and 'moral aims'. There is more than a touch of paternalism about the word 'elite' and it implies a situation in which only a cultivated few really know how to use leisure. The adjective 'professional' further implies that being a member of the elite may itself be a matter of education, such as the gaining of a university degree in professional recreation. The 'moral aims' to be pursued emphasise that only certain kinds of leisure are to be promoted and that they are intended as a means of social control. Indeed, in the sense of seeking to make leisure serve an integrative function in society, the aims of professional recreationists may be seen as holist; it is in their conception of an elitist society and of the mass of people as potential clients of their professional skills that their philosophy is essentially segmentalist.

Holist Policies

In contrast to the kind of policies considered above, holist policies are concerned with the patterning of society as a whole. Although they may embody specific proposals for dealing with work and leisure problems, they do so within a framework of thought that recognises the interdependence of spheres. Indeed, their advocates may go further in suggesting that part of the problem may lie in the very split between spheres and, unlike the advocates of segmentalism, may point to the costs rather than the gains to the individual of such a split. Inevitably their policies are longer term than segmentalist ones, since they involve wider repercussions on established standards of behaviour and values. Segmentalists desire to make 'practical', piecemeal reforms to the existing work–leisure spheres starting with the immediate environments of individuals. Those adopting a holist theory will insist that more far-reaching policies aimed at changes in the social and economic structure as a whole are necessary (Banner, 1974).

Most holist policies for dealing with work and leisure have a basis in work, since those who put them forward tend to share the view that leisure is itself a creation of our industrial system. With this proviso, concepts that apply to both work and leisure have a special place in holist policies. One such concept is the 'productive orientation' put forward by Fromm (1956). This refers to the active and creative relatedness of man to his fellow man, to himself and to nature, and is expressed in the realms of thought, feeling and action. The productive orientation is set against both the exploitative, hoarding orientation (the exploitation of man by man and the pleasure in possession and property, dominant in the nineteenth century) and the receptive and marketing orientation (the passive 'drinking in' of commodities and the experience of oneself as a thing to be employed successfully on the market, dominant today). The receptive and marketing orientation sums up a situation of alienation from both work and leisure. In contrast, the productive orientation sums up a situation in which people participate actively in what they do, whether it is called work or leisure. Such an orientation is implicit in Harrington's (1966) belief that 'there could be a new kind of leisure and a new kind of work, or more precisely a range of activities that would partake of the nature of both leisure and work'.

A number of writers have suggested that one of the chief barriers to a closer integration of work and leisure is the preoccupation of our society with production at the expense of other values, and the individual preference for more income at the expense of more leisure time. Day (1964) has pointed out that much the greater part of the benefit of rising productivity has been taken out in the form of more money to buy more goods, and very little in the form of increased leisure through shorter working hours. Bearing in mind the growth of hire purchase and the power of the mass media to stimulate wants which need higher incomes to satisfy them, there is no reason to look for an early and dramatic reversal of this trend, although more recent evidence from America suggests that income from the job is increasingly being traded for more leisure time (Best, 1980). Day also notes that some of the benefits of technological advance are now enjoyed in the form not of higher productivity but of more pleasant working conditions. Easing off on the job so as to have more time for a smoke or a gossip may constitute a 'restrictive practice' from a purely economic point of view, but may, from the worker's point of view, be a reduction in the split between work (which is something unpleasant and has to be tolerated) and leisure (which is isolated and pleasurable).

Day suggests that rising productivity might allow us to 'deliberately choose methods of production which may not necessarily be the most "efficient" but still contribute most to human happiness'. There is certainly plenty of scope for increasing this contribution to happiness so far as the average worker today is concerned. It is true that considerable progress has been made over the last fifty years in improving the physical environment of the worker. When factories are built nowadays attention is paid to proper lighting, temperature, noise control, ventilation and even decorative colour schemes. Standards in office building and equipment have also improved. These developments have been partly the result of management's awareness that a good working environment promotes efficiency and partly the result of the pressure of organised labour. But even if the standards reached by the best firms today are eventually achieved by the others, all this does not change the content of the work and what it means to the people who have to do it. If the achievements of the past fifty years have been concentrated on the physical environment of work, attention over the next fifty years must turn increasingly to the quality of working life itself – the social relationships of work and the opportunities it gives for personal fulfilment.

It is too often thought to be a matter of little or no importance that most jobs today (or, more precisely, the way they are organised and the conditions under which they are done) afford no satisfaction and are even sources of misery and frustration. Perhaps those responsible for planning and running industry will be forced to turn their attention to improving the experience of work only when other methods of preventing workers from taking 'militant action' through boredom and frustration have failed. With the present high levels of unemployment the advantage is with employers and the political, industrial and commercial establishment: workers are told they are 'lucky to have jobs' and are forced to compete with others for scarce job opportunities. But hopefully this imbalance of power will change and, after the supply of jobs more nearly equates demand, attention will once again turn to improving the quality of working lives.

It is sometimes said that we have put the Victorian 'work morality' behind us because we allow that work need no longer be the sole preoccupation of life. But in another sense this morality lives on. We are continually brainwashed with ideas about increasing productivity, the balance of payments, becoming more competitive, and so on. But none of these things really touches the quality of life of the average man or woman. Are we to go on forever working for the greater glory of the gross national product? Are we to become increasingly the paying customers of the leisure industries? To pose these questions is not to assert that collectively we can consume more than we produce, nor is it to deny the continuing need to harness technical knowledge and scientific advance to the benefit of mankind; but it *is* to challenge the assumption that the present economic and social organisation of our affairs, with its own peculiar priorities, is the most appropriate one to meet our needs.

Imaginative critics of the present order point to the integration of work and leisure now experienced by some employees as something that could be extended to the lives of others. Thus Denbigh (1963) has written: 'Surely it should be one of the important functions of industry in society that the employment it gives should be such that a man

can put into his work a great deal of himself. Professional people take
it for granted that their own work is of this kind.' A holist consideration that the raising of levels of consumption will eventually call into
question the quality of the work environment leads Denbigh to assert
that 'there will surely come a time when the world will want some
new kind of productive system – one which will yield, as well as the
output of goods, more rewarding conditions in their making'. It is
unlikely that 'the world' will suddenly decide it wants such a system.
Much more probably, a growing number of men and women, having
achieved better material standards of living, will turn their attention to
improving their lives in other ways, including demanding for themselves and others working lives worthy of whole persons and not
merely of hired hands.

What do holist policies imply for the actual content and conditions
of work and leisure? Apart from deliberately introducing leisure-like
experiences into the working day (thereby somewhat blurring the
distinction between work and leisure) certain policies with regard to
the organisation of work are also relevant. Greater autonomy in their
own jobs and greater participation in the way the enterprise as a whole
is run are two of the main ways in which holist policies would benefit
employees. Giving people more autonomy in their work should help
to reconcile work with leisure, since this is a feature of jobs that has
been shown to be associated with the extension pattern. Democratic
participation in the running of industrial and commercial enterprises is
important because it is likely to be accompanied by democratic
participation in running the affairs of the community.

It is possible to approach the twin problems of work and leisure
from the angle of leisure as well as that of work. Instead of starting
with concepts such as the 'productive orientation' or 'shared responsibilities', which stem mainly from work, we can inquire what is the
optimum role of leisure in life and society and then seek to integrate
this with other spheres, including work. Leisure as the opposite of
work, that is, leisure as detachment, passivity and general absence of
effort, is not reconcilable with work. But leisure as interest, pleasurable activity and a general sense of creative self-expression can be seen
as continuous with some aspects of work. Our aim can thus include
the growth of leisure time in which to do the work we wish.

Revaluing Work and Leisure

A major difference between segmentalist and holist policies is that the
former deal with the implications of changes in only one segment at a
time, assuming everything else to be constant, whereas the latter deal
with the impact of change in any part of the system on the system as a

whole. Although the field of policy is one in which it would be foolish to deny the role of value judgements about what is desirable, there is a sense in which the very structure of complex social interrelationships determines the extent of repercussions of change initiated at any one point. Segmentalism 'works' to the extent that the spheres of society (or of the individual's life) *are* actually segmented, but it fails to the extent that change in a part affects the whole. These considerations have special relevance to the problem of values attached to work and leisure.

Any revaluation of work and leisure must first of all involve a redefinition of the terms, or at least a change of emphasis in their meaning. In Chapter 3 it was shown that employment is only one kind of work and that, since leisure means choice, time spent from choice in work activity can be leisure just as much as can the more usual leisure activities. By policies which introduce leisure-like elements into employment situations and by a refusal to define leisure as a separate period in which no work is done, the present largely opposite conceptions of work and leisure may be changed in the direction of integration. However, it is not necessary – nor perhaps even desirable – to aim at complete fusion of work and leisure so that they become indistinguishable. As long as there are discrepancies between individual needs or aims and the needs (that is, the best interests) of society as whole, there will continue to be some measure of constraint on at least some of the time of most of the people. The basic distinction between instrumental (means) and expressive (end) activities, and differences in degrees of constraint or choice, will mean that some such terms as work and leisure will continue to have relevance, though probably not such sharply differentiated meanings as they have for most people today. Also, it must not be forgotten that leisure as relative freedom from constraint can be a counter both to work and to non-work obligations. Dumazedier (1967) says:

> Leisure can become a breaking-away in two senses. It is a stoppage of activities required by the job, or family or social responsibilities, and at the same time a sharp questioning of the routine stereotypes and ready-made notions resulting from the repetitiveness and specialization of day-to-day responsibilities. (p. 230)

Although I believe this approach to leisure unduly emphasises its separation from the rest of life, I agree that leisure as a questioning of routine represents a most constructive revaluation.

Two developments in modern industry have implications for a revaluation of work and leisure. The first concerns the change in the occupational structure which has been taking place in recent decades.

Proportionately more people are now engaged in professional and service-type occupations. This change should, in the long run, reduce the proportion of employees who feel alienated from their work. Fried (1966) has shown that the concept of what is work undergoes change as occupations develop in terms of such factors as advanced training, skills and abilities required. At the lowest level, work is just a *job* involving subordination to other people. It may then become a *task* allowing some pleasure and pride in performance. As an *occupation*, work includes not only task-pleasure but also provides opportunities for developing responsibility for, and identity with, an overall integrated work goal. Finally, a *career* may enable people to identify their own personal achievement with their work and to make social participation and individual fulfilment almost indistinguishable. The occupational structure is tending to provide more careers and opportunities for people to have that kind of relationship to their work.

A second development making for a revaluation of work and leisure is the reduction in working hours which the mass of people have already gained and may continue to gain. Estimates of the probable future rate of reduction vary, but few question the direction of the trend. It is mainly these two developments that have led to the claim that, paradoxically, we are clearing the way for meaningful and voluntary work by maximising leisure (Soule, 1956). As technological advances and the growth of service occupations make it more and more difficult to measure the output of a single individual, the purely economic function of work to the employee is called into question. We have already reached the stage when it is becoming increasingly unrealistic to expect everyone to 'pay' for everything he consumes from the income gained by a measured contribution to society. It used to be only the owners of capital who were subsidised by the efforts of working people; today, other non-producers or virtual non-producers are also getting incomes out of all proportion to efforts expended. Our outmoded economic system pays financial geniuses, entertainment superstars, and so on, their absurdly inflated market price, but it also employs machine-minders for machines that do not need minding and clerks for paperwork that could be drastically reduced in a saner system. No wonder that Rhee (1968) asks 'Will not a largely automated, labour-saving, management-saving, organization-saving, post-industrial society of the future find it necessary, first to devise new ways of distributing society's wealth and, secondly, to enable people to enjoy the satisfactions derived from work?' The long-term answer must surely be in the affirmative, and our short-term problem is to see how we can move in that direction.

A third development encouraging the revaluation of work and leisure is the greater role that non-employment work is playing in our socioeconomic pattern of living, or, as Gershuny (1978) describes it, the emergence of the self-service economy. A formal sector corresponding to employment as we know it today will gradually be overshadowed by the informal sector, in which production and consumption activities are based on the same social unit. As this happens, the distinction between work and leisure will become less clear-cut. The complex of activities including recreation, education, housework, and so on, which make up the informal sector will increasingly become a viable alternative to employment in the formal sector, at certain stages in all our lives.

All this assumes a revaluation – indeed a devaluation – of employment. It assumes a redistribution of income, if not of wealth, so that those not in employment at any particular time share reasonable equally in the wealth of the community. Unemployment, redefined in more positive terms as a period of contributing to society or to personal development in ways other than having a paid job, will lose much of its stigma. But other problems of identity and the structuring of life may remain, at least for a time. Employment, despite its negative aspects, provides a structure to life through specifying the time, place and patterns of many of one's activities – including patterns of social relationships imposed by the interdependence of people in their employment situation (Kelvin, 1981). It is particularly this structure of stable social relationships which is so widely and greatly missed when people become unemployed or retire. With a set of values oriented to work in the formal sector, few leisure activities are seen as demanding and affording the personal and interpersonal satisfactions of work. To paraphrase Green (1968), while the concept of leisure is opposed to that of job or employment, it is not opposed to the idea of having a work to do, that is, a creative activity – short-term, or perhaps extending over a lifetime – which entails personal commitment and provides satisfaction, fulfilment and a sense of identity.

Alternative Scenarios

From its original musical meaning, the term 'scenario' has been widened to include summary descriptions of possible futures. Scenarios are useful because they enable us to predict what will happen if existing trends continue, but they also seek to take account of cyclical or even unpredictable changes, in either material circumstances or influential social values.

The simplest form of scenario is an extrapolation into the future of a one-dimensional trend: for example, the supposition that we shall have an average of 10 hours employment a week in 100 years' time because today we average 40 hours and 100 years ago we averaged 70 hours. Of course, such predictions rarely come true because the rate of change, even if the change continues in the same direction, is affected by intervening and often unforeseen variables or happenings.

In trying to construct alternative scenarios concerning leisure and work we may pay most attention to continuities, to discontinuities, or to some mixture of the two. In terms of goals, we may posit work as primary, leisure as primary, or both as being of equal importance. Most recently proposed scenarios ignore work alone as a main goal of life, perhaps because we are still reacting to a period of history when this was the dominant theme. Miles and his colleagues (1978), for example, describe two 'images of the future': one leisure-oriented and one giving equal weight to work and leisure:

> One view sees leisure as the goal of economic development and technological change. The goal is not merely to have maximum free time and earned income (or production), which will enable one to fill such time with agreeable (or fulfilling) activities. This suggests the image of a highly automated society in which jobs have been mechanised so that they make diminishing demands on time, skill or patience, and the major part of one's life is spent in intrinsically satisfying recreation. An alternative view, however, sees both work and leisure as having the potential to be intrinsically satisfying activities; both are possible routes to personal and social development, and mutually supportive. (p. 335)

Other scenarios attempt to bring more variables into the picture, for example, treating as problematic the division of the population into workers and consumers. Thus for Johnston (1972) there are three alternative scenarios. The first is of an automated society in which a small number of people would be responsible for production and distribution of goods, with the remainder of the population limited to consumption. The corresponding ethic would be a takeover by leisure of the intrinsic and personally satisfying aspects of life, with work being accepted primarily for the monetary reward it brings. The second scenario recognises the realisation and maintenance of a full-employment economy and assumes the maintenance of the work ethic, with a steady flow of appropriately trained persons willing to work. The third scenario suggests a gradual reunification of work and leisure into a holistic pattern characteristic of most pre-industrial societies. The economic sector would be linked more closely to non-economic forces, so that non-material cultural values would tend to become the primary determinants of what we produce and consume.

One of the most challenging of recent attempts at scenario building is that of Martin and Mason (1982). Their alternatives represent combinations of national economic success or failure with different views of what might happen to social values. The first scenario ('conventional success') would result from a rapid and sustained rate of economic growth accompanied by conventional attitudes to work and leisure ('work hard, play hard'), with leisure seen as a time for rest, recuperation and entertainment. Secondly, 'frustration' could be produced by lack of economic growth and conventional attitudes to work and leisure (leisure seen by many as an escape from harsh reality). Thirdly, a high level of economic growth and changed social attitudes could constitute 'transformed growth' (a positive attitude to leisure reflecting personal and social development). Finally, no economic growth but changed attitudes could produce 'self restraint' (reduced distinction between work and leisure). Martin and Mason flesh out their scenarios with much speculative detail, but some of the references to economic policies are rather too conventional to establish the authors as convincing apostles of changed attitudes to work and leisure.

The Role of Education

The processes of work and leisure revaluation and of attempting to change social institutions and behaviour according to preferred scenarios rely heavily on education – indeed, it is no exaggeration to say that education is the key institution in these processes. We should be concerned not just with what is taught in schools but also with what is learned by individuals in various ways throughout the whole of their lives. To advocate the teaching of 'leisure' subjects to young people who, if they find employment at all, are not likely to make it their central life interest is a short-term, segmentalist answer. From a holist point of view we need subjects to be taught in such a way that they are exclusive neither to work nor to leisure.

Education is, by tradition and in theory, a leisure activity (Peterson, 1975). The word 'school' is etymologically associated with leisure and the belief that learning should be pursued for its own sake is a cliché of the educational theorist and of the prize-giving address; yet the activity is commonly referred to as 'school work'. This contradiction now serves to sustain the separate worlds of teaching marketable skills (training) and developing understanding of ourselves and the world in which we live (true education). The contradiction could, however, take on a more dialectical character: challenging contemporary values of work with those of classical leisure and questioning contemporary values of leisure by reference to work in its most creative and pleasurable forms.

It is more than just wishful thinking to expect that, as the demands of work in terms of time and effort are reduced, individuals will look for more facilities to improve their own knowledge (Thornton and Wheelock, 1979). The success of the Open University, notwithstanding the career motives of many of its students, demonstrates this need. While the work ethic is gradually weakening, there will remain the fundamental human need to feel useful. The transition will require new definitions of work and social usefulness. Education has a dual role to play in this process – as a means of preparing men and women for more leisure and as itself a leisure time activity.

Another role of education in promoting changed work–leisure relationships is to enable people to gain a better understanding of the nature of the changes taking place in their society and to encourage them to play an active part in further changes. As Vickerman (1980) points out, the greatest inequities are essentially informational ones. We have the opportunity, as never before, to create non-material wealth, but unless it is geared to general welfare rather than to the free market economy the new Renaissance for the few will mean a new Dark Age for the many. At the level of the individual, we should be looking for a reintegration of work and leisure through self-directed education (Gotlieb and Borodin, 1973).

Planning for Work and Leisure

If the realisation of human potentialities in work and leisure is to be pursued as a social aim, there arises the question of how the relevant policies may be shaped and administered and what part sociologists can play in this. It is true, as Bressler (1961) points out, that 'sociologists *qua* sociologists have no special gifts as definers of public welfare'. However, this does not mean that sociological theory and research has nothing to contribute to policy-making. Within industry sociologists can convey to management, unions and employees the results and conclusions of investigations into the effects of variables in the work situation (such as authority structure, type of technology and style of supervision) on workers' attitudes. Those in a position to initiate or press for changes in these respects may do so in the reasonable expectation that corresponding changes will result. In the realm of leisure, sociologists can obtain and convey to both the consumers and the providers of leisure goods and services information concerning the needs of people in various situations and the factors which have combined to produce those needs. Even more important, sociologists can join with psychologists, philosophers, historians, economists, administrators and others in making the general public more aware of the possibilities of *social* development that technological development is opening up. Substantial numbers of students and organised workers are showing increasing militancy in seeking some degree of control over the conditions of their educational and working lives. These campaigns may be seen as the spearhead of a wider movement towards a type of society which not only allows but positively encourages democratic participation by all its members.

Any programme for the realisation of human potentialities must be based on the satisfaction of need, but the concept of need may be interpreted in various ways. Needs vary from the purely physiological to the most socially determined. Some needs are basic to life itself and their satisfaction occupies an irreducible minimum of any individual's time budget. At the other end of the scale are needs which are least basic but are said to express most fully the character of civilised man (Maslow, 1954). Just as individuals have to satisfy their basic needs before they can concern themselves with 'higher things', so society has first to meet the basic needs of all its members before it can provide leisure for more than a privileged few of them. But to see a straight-line progression from all labour (distinguished from both work and leisure, in Arendt's sense) to all leisure is to distort the picture. The weight of historical, anthropological and contemporary evidence is that, whatever their expressed desires, men and women in all societies must have work as well as leisure. Further, for people whose work embodies many of the values normally associated with leisure, a separate period of time labelled leisure does not appear to be necessary either to their own happiness or to their creative function in society.

The central problem, then, is not one of maximising some values (that is, those associated with leisure) and minimising others (associated with work) but of achieving an integration of both sets of values. Integration of another kind is also necessary: that between the needs of individuals and of society. It is this latter kind of integration that poses the most problems to those concerned with planning for work and leisure, since it is only in a metaphorical sense that society has 'needs' apart from those of its individual members. Neither the needs for work nor those for leisure are easy to determine on a societal scale, and the latter kind are particularly difficult. It is fairly easy to see what kinds of work fulfil expressive needs, because the kinds of work that do not are undertaken only instrumentally. But with leisure there is no such criterion to employ – it is all supposed to be expressive.

Willener (1967) writes that 'true leisure ought to be free, "natural", it cannot be engineered'. This is the *laissez-faire* doctrine of leisure as free time, apparently not determined by anyone other than the leisure-user himself, but in fact quite markedly mediated by various social influences, for example, those of the mass media and of advertisers. It is true that the person who is sufficiently self-contained or inner-directed may resist these influences and, provided he has resources developed in other spheres of life, create for himself an autonomous leisure. But for the mass of people who play no greater part in determining the conditions of their leisure than they do in determining the conditions of their work, the choice is not whether their use of leisure is engineered or not; the choice is between having it engineered by various agencies, with various degrees of persuasive power and with various motives on the part of those doing the persuading (Glasser, 1970). At present we appear to be content to let the provision of leisure facilities, and even the very ideas about how leisure should be spent, be guided by a kind of 'invisible hand', which produces in the leisure field results comparable to those produced by the same *laissez-faire* doctrine in the industrial field. Social improvements do not just come about. Priorities have to be determined and efforts for their achievement must be kept up.

There is surely a parallel to be drawn between planning in the industrial sphere and planning in the leisure sphere. The recognition that unregulated *laissez-faire* is not the best way to reconcile supply and demand, even within a market economy, led to the intervention of the state and its increasingly important role as supreme planner. However, in Western countries the role of the state is limited and decisions at a lower level than those of national policy are left in the hands of individuals or groups, though these decisions are to a large extent shaped by the interplay of economic factors and not by individual will. The parallel with leisure lies in the possibility of state or other collective intervention in decisions which affect the facilities and opportunities provided for leisure, but in such a way that individual autonomy and development would be promoted rather than diminished.

Most of us would agree that we should not try to direct people's energies into channels specified in advance. We should aim instead to nourish the individual's potentialities so that each, according to his capacity, can find his own solution. Unfortunately, as Aron (1968) points out, 'all societies, including the wealthiest, continue to train *the men they need* but ... none, despite its proclaimed objectives, *needs* to have all men realize fully their individual potentialities. No society *needs* to have many men become personalities fully capable of freedom in relation to their environment'. The message is plain enough: if we do not press for opportunities to realise our individual potentialities, no one else is going to do it for us. This especially goes for working life – neither the government, nor the employers, nor even the trade unions, are there to develop us as persons. Various pressure groups may be made, at least partially, to serve this end but the impetus must come from ourselves.

Traditional land-use planning considered that leisure was the luxury of the few and that for the masses work came first and whatever was left over was free time to be passed as 'wholesomely' – and as cheaply to the community – as possible. Such a concept of planning survives today and concentrates on the requirements of the work environment, giving high priority to efficient physical relationships among factories, offices, schools, shops, houses and transport routes. The residual 'open space' that remains has too often been regarded as adequate to meet leisure requirements. Planners have paid very little attention to a positive approach to leisure by understanding and forecasting trends in leisure-time behaviour, although there has in recent years been some growth in setting up mechanisms for public participation in local environment decisions. Moreover, there has been almost no concern with how demand is shaped – planning has taken notice of vested interests and pressure groups but not of what might be called the needs for individual, personal development.

Finally, we may consider a further aspect of the role of the sociologist in planning for work and leisure. It has already been noted that, in providing certain facts about human needs and satisfactions, sociologists and others may indirectly influence those having some responsibility for the way people work and spend their leisure time. At this level the role of values may be kept fairly neutral. It need not be a matter of saying 'we want you to make these changes because we think they would be good for people'. The advice may be limited to the relatively value-free type of '*If* you do this, *then* that is likely to result'. The qualification 'relatively' is necessary because the selection of a course of action the results of which are to be predicted itself represents a priority choice from among a number of possible courses of action.

Apart from this type of dispassionate advice, there are the methods of 'active sociology' which some sociologists advocate. Active sociology

> holds that the social subject, though determined by a situation, has at the same time the power to determine the situation by a conscious and voluntary policy . . . it is not a question of conducting a historical study of the past but of selecting, from among all the processes of evolution, those which correspond to explicit criteria of development and of making a prognosis of their probable projection in the short or long term, according to one or more possible courses of action. (Samuel, 1967, p. 1)

'Criteria of development' clearly imply a value-choice, but once selected they can lead on to a more strictly sociological process of analysing the nature of the interaction of various social forces. Thus leisure may be seen as 'a factor for cultural progress or cultural decline, for social integration or alienation, it may stimulate the involvement of the individual or lead him into irresponsibility towards himself and his kind'. We may first choose which of these alternatives we think preferable, analyse its sources and manifestations and then take appropriate action to achieve the desired ends. A similar procedure may be followed with regard to work.

Conclusion

Most of this book has been devoted to showing that there are types of relationship between work and leisure to be seen on the levels both of individual life spheres and of social organisation. To attribute the main reason for these different relationships either to types of person or to types of social situation has important implications for policy. In the one case attempts will be made to fit persons seeking (or not seeking) fulfilment in work to jobs capable (or incapable) of providing that fulfilment. In the other case attempts will be made, through more far-reaching changes, to give everyone the chance of experiencing similar encouragement to development through work. In the field of leisure the one policy will be to provide leisure facilities for the 'type of people' who need them; the other policy to stimulate an awareness of the possibilities of leisure-like behaviour in a variety of situations – including work.

The choice between two main schools of thought about the relationship of life spheres in urban-industrial society is also important. Segmentalists will want to tackle the problems of work and leisure in relative isolation from each other, on the assumption that differentiation of spheres makes this possible; holists will want to pursue a more difficult and longer-term policy of integration, on the assumption that the interdependence of spheres makes this necessary. At the level of general theories of society there are again implications for policy. Segmentalists will want to make 'practical' reforms to the existing work and leisure spheres starting with the experiences and immediate environments of individuals. Holists will insist that more far-reaching policies aimed at changes in the social and economic structure as a whole are necessary.

Any specific changes in the content, organisation and environment of work and leisure will depend for their success on accompanying changes in the relevant social values or philosophy (Maklan, 1977). The key institution in any process of revaluation is education, both in the schools and in adult life. In the schools boys and girls may be taught in such a way that subjects are not regarded as 'vocational' and 'non-vocational' (narrowly vocational subjects are, in any case, training rather than education) and then encouraged to expect more from any job they choose than just the pay packet. There must, of course, be a reasonable balance between the number and types of job-seeker and the number and types of job to be made available, although not to be in employment while learning, or having leisure, or doing useful community or social work, may also be accepted as the norm at some variable stages of life.

It may be that some men and women will still choose to invest relatively little of themselves in work and may see it only as a means to enjoying leisure – but at least the options will have been open. Collective action to achieve, beyond better pay and conditions, more rewarding work for all would reinforce the process of critical evaluation started in the schools. In the field of leisure provision, the consumer – or rather, the participant – would be encouraged to expect something more than routine diversion, though this should not imply an indiscriminate bias against popular entertainment and in favour of 'high culture'. The important thing is to make available opportunities for rewarding work and for the various kinds of leisure that complement rewarding work. The extent to which advantage is taken of such opportunities must, of course, remain the choice of the individual.

Bibliography

Allen, R. E., and Hawes, D. K. (1979), 'Attitudes toward work, leisure and the four day workweek', *Human Resource Management*, Spring, pp. 5–10.

Anderson, R. (1975), *Leisure.– an Inappropriate Concept for Women*, Department of Tourism and Recreation (Canberra: Australian Government Publishing Service).

Arendt, H. (1958), *The Human Condition* (Chicago: University of Chicago Press).

Argyle, M. (1972), *The Social Psychology of Work* (Harmondsworth: Penguin).

Aron, R. (1962), 'On leisure in industrial societies', in J. Brooks *et al.* (eds), *The One and the Many: The Individual in the Modern World* (New York: Harper & Row), pp. 157–72.

Aron, R. (1968), *Progress and Disillusion: The Dialectics of Modern Society* (London: Pall Mall).

Ashton, H. (1967), *The Basuto* (London: Oxford University Press).

Atchley, R. (1971) 'Retirement and leisure participation: continuity or crisis?', *Gerontologist*, vol. 11 (Spring).

Bacon, A. W. (1972a), 'Leisure and research: a critical review of the main concepts employed in contemporary research', *Society and Leisure*, no. 2, pp. 83–92.

Bacon, A. W. (1972b), 'The embarrassed self: some reflections upon attitudes to work and idleness in a prosperous industrial society', *Society and Leisure*, no. 4.

Bacon, A. W. (1975), 'Leisure and the alienated worker: a critical reassessment of three radical theories of work and leisure', *Journal of Leisure Research*, vol. 7, no. 3, pp. 179–90.

Bacon, A. W. (1977), 'Leisure and the craftworkers', in M. A. Smith (ed.), *Leisure and Urban Society* (London: Leisure Studies Association).

Bailey, P. (1978), *Leisure and Class in Victorian England* (London: Routledge & Kegan Paul).

Banner, D. K. (1974), 'The nature of the work–leisure relationship', *Omega*, vol. 2, no. 2, pp. 181–95.

Barnes, H. E., and Ruedi, O. M. (1950), *The American Way of Life* (New York: Prentice-Hall).

Barron, I., and Curnow, R. (1979), *The Future with Microelectronics* (London: Pinter).

Beauvoir, S. de (1972), *Old Age* (London: Deutsch).

Bell, D. (1954), 'Work in the life of an American', in W. Haber *et al.* (eds), *Manpower in the United States* (New York: Harper & Row), pp. 3–22.

Berger, P. (1964), *The Human Shape of Work* (New York: Macmillan).

Bernal, J. D. (1939), *The Social Function of Science* (London: Routledge & Kegan Paul).

Best, F. (1980), *Exchanging Earnings for Leisure: Findings of an Exploratory National Survey on Work Time Preferences* (Washington, DC: US Government Printing Office).

Bishop, D. W., and Ikeda, M. (1970), 'Status and role factors in the leisure behaviour of different occupations', *Sociology and Social Research*, vol. 54, no. 2, pp. 190–208.

Blakelock, E. H. (1961), 'A Durkheimian approach to some temporal problems of leisure', *Social Problems*, Summer, pp. 9–16.

Blau, P. M., and Scott, W. R. (1963), *Formal Organizations* (London: Routledge & Kegan Paul).

Blauner, R. (1964), *Alienation and Freedom* (Chicago: University of Chicago Press).

Blum, F. H. (1953), *Toward a Democratic Work Process* (New York: Harper & Row).

Boggs, S. T. (1963), 'The values of laboratory workers', *Human Organization*, Fall, pp. 207–15.

Bressler, M. (1961), 'Some selected aspects of American sociology', *Annals of the American Academy of Political and Social Science*, September, pp. 146–59.

Brightbill, C. K. (1963), *The Challenge of Leisure* (Englewood Cliffs, NJ: Prentice-Hall).

British Travel Association/University of Keele (1967), *Pilot National Recreation Survey – Report No. 1*, July.

Brown, R. (1973), 'Leisure in work: the "occupational culture" of shipbuilding workers', in M. A. Smith *et al.* (eds), *Leisure and Society in Britain* (London: Allen Lane), pp. 97–110.

Brutzkus, E. (1980), 'Technological advance beyond the optimum', *Ekistics*, vol. 47 (September), pp. 384–9.

Burawoy, M. (1978), 'Toward a Marxist theory of the labour process: Braverman and beyond', *Politics and Society*, vol. 8, no. 3, pp. 267–312.

Burch, W. R. (1971), 'Images of future leisure: continuities in changing expectations', in W. Bell and A. Mau (eds), *The Sociology of the Future* (New York: Russell Sage), pp. 160–87.

Burns, T. (1967), 'A meaning in everyday life', *New Society*, 25 May.

Burns, T., and Stalker, G. M. (1961), *The Management of Innovation* (London: Tavistock).

Central Policy Review Staff (1978), *Social and Economic Implications of Microelectronics* (London: HMSO).

Cheek, N. H., and Burch, W. R. (1976), *The Social Organization of Leisure in Human Society* (New York: Harper & Row).

Chisholm, R. F. (1978), 'The web of work for technical and managerial employees', *Journal of Vocational Behaviour*, vol. 13, pp. 101–12.

Clarke, A. C. (1956), 'The use of leisure and its relation to levels of occupational prestige', *American Sociological Review*, June, pp. 301–7.

Clayre, A. (1974), *Work and Play* (London: Weidenfeld & Nicolson).

Coalter, F. (1982), 'Workshop report: unemployment', in A. J. Veal *et al.* (eds), *Work and Leisure* (London: Leisure Studies Association).

Coles, L. (1980), 'Women and leisure – a critical perspective', in D. Mercer and E. Hamilton-Smith (eds), *Recreation Planning and Social Change in Urban Australia* (Malvern, Australia: Sorrett), pp. 63–73.

Corrigan, P. (1982), 'The trouble with being unemployed is that you never get a day off', in A. J. Veal *et al.* (eds), *Work and Leisure* (London: Leisure Studies Association).

Council for Science and Society (1981), *New Technology: Society, Employment and Skill* (London: CSS).

Cunningham, H. (1980), *Leisure in the Industrial Revolution* (London: Croom Helm).

Dale, R., and Williamson, I. (1980), *The Myth of the Micro* (London: W. H. Allen).

Day, A. (1964), 'Leisure for living', *Observer*, 17 May.

Deem, R. (1982), 'Women, leisure and inequality', *Leisure Studies*, vol. 1 (January), pp. 29–46.

DeGrazia, S. (1962), *Of Time, Work and Leisure* (New York: Twentieth Century Fund).

Denbigh, K. (1963), *Science, Industry and Social Policy* (Edinburgh: Oliver & Boyd).

Donald, M. N., and Havighurst, R. J. (1959), 'The meanings of leisure', *Social Forces*, May, pp. 335–9.

Dubin, R. (1956), 'Industrial workers' worlds', *Social Problems*, January, pp. 131–43.

Dubin, R. (1963), personal correspondence.

Dubin, R., Hedley, R. A., and Taveggia, T. C. (1976), 'Attachment to work', in R. Dubin (ed), *Handbook of Work, Organization and Society* (Chicago: Rand McNally).

Duff, A., and Cotgrove, S. (1982), 'Social values and the choice of careers in industry', *Journal of Occupational Psychology*, vol. 55 (June), pp. 97–108.

Dumazedier, J. (1960), 'Current problems of the sociology of leisure', *International Social Science Journal*, no. 4, pp. 522–31.

Dumazedier, J. (1967), *Toward a Society of Leisure* (London: Collier Macmillan).

Dumazedier, J., and Latouche, N. (1962) 'Work and leisure in French sociology', *Industrial Relations*, February.

Durant, H. W. (1938), *The Problem of Leisure* (London: Routledge & Kegan Paul).

Eldridge, J. E. T. (1971), *Sociology and Industrial Life* (London: Michael Joseph).

Ellul, J. (1965), *The Technological Society* (London: Cape).

Encel, S. (1980), 'The changing character of working life', *Tertiary and Further Education Quarterly* (Australia), Autumn, p. 22.

Ennis, P. H. (1968), 'The definition and measurement of leisure', in E. B. Sheldon and W. E. Moore (eds), *Indicators of Social Change* (New York: Russell Sage).

Etzioni, A. (1961), *A Comparative Analysis of Complex Organizations* (New York: The Free Press).

Etzkorn, K. P. (1964), 'Leisure and camping: the social meaning of a form of public recreation', *Sociology and Social Research*, October, pp. 76–89.

Evans, C. (1979), *The Mighty Micro: The Impact of the Computer* (London: Gollancz).

Fairchild, H. P. (1944), *Dictionary of Sociology* (New York: Philosophical Library).

Faunce, W. A. (1959), 'Automation and leisure', in H. B. Jacobson and J. C. Roucek (eds), *Automation and Society* (New York: Philosophical Library).

Forester, T. (1976), 'The new depression', *New Society*, 5 February, pp. 265–8.

Forte, S. (1979), 'Microelectronics in a nutshell', *Personnel Management*, vol. 11, May, pp. 26–9.

Fraser, J. M. (1962), *Industrial Psychology* (Oxford: Pergamon Press).

Fraser, R. (ed) (1968–9), *Work: Twenty Personal Accounts*, Vols 1 and 2 (Harmonsworth: Penguin).

Fried, M. A. (1966), 'Is work a career?', *Trans-action*, September.

Friedlander, F. (1966), 'Importance of work versus nonwork among socially and occupationally stratified groups', *Journal of Applied Psychology*, December, pp. 437–41.

Friedmann, E. A. (1958), 'The work of leisure', in W. Donahue *et al.* (eds), *Free Time: Challenge to Later Maturity* (Ann Arbor, Mich.: University of Michigan Press).

Friedmann, E. A., and Havighurst, R. J. (1954), *The Meaning of Work and Retirement* (Chicago: University of Chicago Press).

Friedmann, G. (1960), 'Leisure and technological civilization', *International Social Science Journal*, no. 4, pp. 509–21.

Friedmann, G. (1961), *The Anatomy of Work* (London: Heinemann).

Fromm, E. (1956), *The Sane Society* (London: Routledge & Kegan Paul).

Gardell, B. (1976), 'Reactions at work and their influence on non-work activities', *Human Relations*, vol. 29, no. 9, pp. 885–904.

General Household Survey, 1977 (1979) (London: HMSO).

Gershuny, J. (1978), *After Industrial Society? The Emerging Self-Service Economy* (London: Macmillan).

Gershuny, J. (1979) 'The informal economy: its role in post-industrial society', *Futures*, vol. 11 (February), pp. 3–15.

Gerstl, J. E. (1961), 'Leisure taste and occupational milieu', *Social Problems*, Summer, pp. 56–68.

Gerstl, J. E., and Hutton, S. P. (1966), *Engineers: The Anatomy of a Profession* (London: Tavistock).

Giddens, A. (1964), 'Notes on the concept of play and leisure', *Sociological Review*, March, pp. 73–89.

Gist, N. P., and Fava, S. F. (1964), *Urban Society* (New York: Crowell).

Glasser, R. (1970), *Leisure – Penalty or Prize?* (London: Macmillan).

Glyptis, S. A. (1981), 'Leisure life-styles', *Regional Studies*, vol. 15, no. 5, pp. 311–26.

Glyptis, S. A., and Chambers, D. A. (1982), 'No place like home', *Leisure Studies* vol. 1 (September), pp. 247–62.

Godbey, G. (1975), 'Anti-leisure and public recreation policy', in S. Parker *et al.* (eds), *Sport and Leisure in Contemporary Society* (London: Leisure Studies Association), pp. 46–52.

Godbey, G. (1981), *Leisure in Your Life – An Exploration* (Philadelphia, Pa: Saunders).

Goodman, P. (1962), 'Work and leisure', in M. Philipson (ed.), *Automation* (New York: Random House).

Gotlieb, C. C., and Borodin, A. (1973), *Social Issues in Computing* (London: Academic Press).

Graham, S. (1959), 'Social correlates of adult leisure-time behaviour', in M. B. Sussman (ed), *Community Structure and Analysis* (New York: Crowell), pp. 331–54.

Green, T. F. (1968), *Work, Leisure and the American Schools* (New York: Random House).

Gregory, S. (1982), 'Women among others: another view', *Leisure Studies*, vol. 1 (January), pp. 47–52.

Gross, E. (1961) 'A functional approach to leisure analysis', *Social Problems*, Summer, pp. 2–8.

Grubb, E. A. (1975), 'Assembly line boredom and individual differences in recreation participation', *Journal of Leisure Research*, vol. 7, no. 4.

Gunter, B. G., and Gunter, N. C. (1980), 'Leisure styles: a conceptual framework for modern leisure', *Sociological Quarterly*, vol. 21 (Summer, pp. 361–74.

Gupta, N., and Beehr, T. A. (1981), 'Relationships among employees' work and nonwork responses', *Journal of Occupational Behaviour*, vol. 2, no. 3.

Harrington, M. (1966) *The Accidental Century* (London: Weidenfeld & Nicolson).

Havighurst, R. J. (1957), 'The leisure activities of the middle aged', *American Journal of Sociology*, vol. 63 (September), pp. 152–62.

Havighurst, R. J. (1961), 'The nature and values of meaningful free-time activity', in R. W. Kleemeier (ed.), *Aging and Leisure* (New York: Oxford University Press), pp. 309–44.

Havighurst, R. J., and Feigenbaum, K. (1959), 'Leisure and life-style', *American Journal of Sociology*, vol. 64 (January), pp. 396–404.

Heckscher, A. (1963), *The Public Happiness* (London: Hutchinson).

Heckscher, A., and DeGrazia, S. (1959), 'Executive leisure', *Harvard Business Review*, July, pp. 6–18.

Heinze, R. G., and Olk, T. (1982), 'Development of the informal economy', *Futures*, vol. 14 (June), pp. 189–204.

Hill, J. (1978), 'The psychological impact of unemployment', *New Society*, 19 January.

Hochschild, A. R. (1973), *The Unexpected Community* (Englewood Cliffs, NJ: Prentice-Hall).

Hollander, P. (1966), 'Leisure as an American and Soviet value', *Social Problems*, Fall, pp. 179–88.

Howe, I. (1948), 'Notes on mass culture', *Politics*, Spring, pp. 120–3.

Hull, D. (1980) 'The Committee of Inquiry into Technological Change in Australia', commentary on the report of the Committee, Canberra (mimeo).

Hunter, G. (1961), *Work and Leisure* (London: Central Committee of Study Groups).

Jahoda, M. (1979), 'The psychological meanings of unemployment', *New Society*, 6 September, pp. 492–5.

Jenkins, C., and Sherman, B. (1979), *The Collapse of Work* (London: Eyre Methuen).

Jenkins, C., and Sherman, B. (1981), *The Leisure Shock* (London: Eyre Methuen).

Johnston, D. F. (1972), 'The future of work: three possible alternatives', *Monthly Labor Review*, vol. 95 (May).

Kabanoff, B. (1980), 'Work and nonwork: a review of models, methods and findings', *Psychological Bulletin*, vol. 88, no. 1, pp. 60–77.

Kabanoff, B., and O'Brien, G. E. (1980), 'Work and leisure: a task attributes analysis', *Journal of Applied Psychology*, vol. 65 (October), pp. 596–609.

Kando, M. (1975), *Leisure and Popular Culture in Transition* (Saint Louis, Mo.: Mosby).

Kando, T., and Summers, W. (1971), 'The impact of work on leisure', *Pacific Sociological Review*, vol. 14 (July).

Kaplan, M. (1975), *Leisure: Theory and Policy* (New York: Wiley).

Karasek, R. A. (1981), 'Job socialization and job strain', in B. Gardell and G. Johansson (eds), *Working Life* (Chichester: Wiley).

Keenan, J. 'On the dole', in R. Fraser (ed.), *Work: Twenty Personal Accounts* (Harmondsworth: Penguin), pp. 271–9.

Kelly, J. R. (1976), 'Leisure as compensation for work constraint', *Society and Leisure*, vol. 8, no. 3, pp. 73–82.

Kelly, J. R. (1982), *Leisure* (Englewood Cliffs, NJ: Prentice-Hall).

Kelvin, P. (1981), 'Work as a source of identity: the implications of unemployment', *British Journal of Guidance and Counselling*, vol. 9 (January).

Keniston, K. (1962), 'Social change and youth in America', *Daedalus*, Winter, pp. 145–71.

Klausner, W. J. (1968), 'An experiment in leisure', *Science Journal*, June.

Kornhauser, A. (1965), *Mental Health of the Industrial Worker* (New York: Wiley).

Kraus, R. (1978), *Recreation and Leisure in Modern Society* (Santa Monica, Calif.: Goodyear).

Lafitte, P. (1958), *Social Structure and Personality in the Factory* (London: Routledge & Kegan Paul).

Lansbury, R. (1974), 'Careers, work and leisure among the new professionals', *Sociological Review*, vol. 22, no. 3, pp. 385–400.

Laver, M. (1980), *Computers and Social Change* (Cambridge: Cambridge University Press).

Lee, A. McClung (1966), *Multivalent Man* (New York: Braziller).

Linder, S. (1970), *The Harried Leisure Class* (New York: Columbia University Press).

Loizos, P. (1980), 'Images of man', in J. Cherfas and R. Lewin (eds), *Not Work Alone* (London: Temple Smith).

London, M., Crandall, R., and Seals, G. W. (1977), 'The contribution of job and leisure satisfaction to quality of life', *Journal of Applied Psychology*, vol. 62, no. 3, pp. 328–34.

Lowerson, J., and Myerscough, J. (1977), *Time to Spare in Victorian England* (Hassocks: Harvester Press).

Lundberg, G., Komarovsky, M., and McInery, D. (1934), *Leisure – a Suburban Study* (New York: Columbia University Press).

McIntosh, S. (1981), 'Leisure studies and women', in A. Tomlinson (ed), *Leisure and Social Control* (Brighton: Brighton Polytechnic).

McLuhan, M. (1964), *Understanding Media* (London: Routledge & Kegan Paul).

Maklan, D. M. (1977), *The Four-Day Workweek: Blue Collar Adjustment to a Nonconventional Arrangement of Work and Leisure Time* (New York: Praeger).

Mansfield, R., and Evans, M. G. (1975), 'Work and non-work in two occupational groups', *Industrial Relations Journal*, vol. 6, no. 2, pp. 48–54.

Marcuse, H. (1962), *Eros and Civilization* (New York: Vintage Books).

Marcuse, H. (1964), *One Dimensional Man* (London: Routledge & Kegan Paul).

Marsh, P. (1981), *The Silicon Chip Book* (London: Sphere).

Martin, J. (1978), *The Wired Society* (Englewood Cliffs, NJ: Prentice-Hall).

Martin, J., and Norman, A. (1970) *The Computerized Society* (Englewood Cliffs), NJ: Prentice-Hall).

Martin, W., and Mason, S. (1982), *Leisure and Work: the Choices for 1991 and 2001* (Sudbury, Suffolk: Leisure Consultants).

Maslow, A. (1954), *Motivation and Personality* (New York: Harper & Row).

Meissner, M. (1971), 'The long arm of the job: a study of work and leisure', *Industrial Relations*, vol. 10, pp. 239–60.

Mesthene, E. G. (1969), 'Technology and human values', *Science Journal*, vol. 5 (October).

Miles, I., Cole, S., and Gershuny, J. (1978), 'Images of the future', in C. Freeman and M. Jahoda (eds), *World Futures* (Oxford: Martin Robertson), pp. 279–342.

Morse, N., and Weiss, R. (1955), 'The function and meaning of work and the job', *American Sociological Review*, April, pp. 191–8.

Moss, L., and Parker, S. (1967), *The Local Government Councillor* (London: HMSO).

Murphy, J. F. (1974), *Concepts of Leisure* (Englewood Cliffs, NJ: Prentice-Hall).

Musolino, R. F., and Hershenon, D. B. (1977), 'Avocational sensation seeking in high and low risk-taking occupations', *Journal of Vocational Behaviour*, vol. 10, pp. 358–65.

Near, J. P., Rice, R. W., and Hunt, R. G. (1980), 'The relationship between work and nonwork domains: a review of empirical research', *Academy of Management Review*, vol. 5, no. 3, pp. 415–30.

Noe, F. P. (1970), 'A comparative typology of leisure in non-industrialized society', *Journal of Leisure Research*, vol. 2.

Odaka, K. (1966), 'Work and leisure: as viewed by Japanese industrial workers', paper presented to Sixth World Congress of Sociology, Evian.

Orzack, L. (1959), 'Work as a "central life interest" of professionals', *Social Problems*, Fall, pp. 125–32.

Orpen, C. (1978), 'Work and nonwork satisfaction: a causal-correlational analysis', *Journal of Applied Psychology*, vol. 63, pp. 530–2.

Palm, G. (1977), *The Flight from Work* (Cambridge: Cambridge University Press).

Parker, S. (1968), 'Work and leisure: a study of their interrelation', PhD thesis, University of London.

Parker, S. (1981), 'Choice, flexibility, spontaneity and self-determination in leisure', *Social Forces*, December, pp. 323–31.

Parker, S. (1982), *Work and Retirement* (London: Allen & Unwin).

Peppers, L. F. (1976), 'Patterns of leisure and adjustment to retirement', *Gerontologist*, vol. 16 (October), pp. 441–6.

Peterson, A. D. C. (1975), 'Education for work or for leisure?', in J. T. Haworth and M. A. Smith (eds), *Work and Leisure* (London: Lepus).

Pieper, J. (1952), *Leisure the Basis of Culture* (London: Faber).

Pym, D. (1979), 'Work is good, employment is bad', *Employee Relations*, vol. 1, no. 1.

Rapoport, R., and Rapoport, R. N. (1975), *Leisure and the Family Life Cycle* (London: Routledge & Kegan Paul).

Reissman, L. (1954), 'Class, leisure and social participation', *American Sociological Review*, February, pp. 76–84.

Rhee, H. (1968), *Office Automation in Social Perspective* (Oxford: Blackwell).

Rice, R. W., Near, J. P., and Hunt, R. G. (1979), 'Unique variance in job and life satisfaction associated with work-related and extra-workplace variables', *Human Relations*, vol. 32 (July), pp. 605–24.

Riesman, D. (1952), 'Some observations on changes in leisure attitudes', *Antioch Review*, no. 4.

Riesman, D. (1953), *The Lonely Crowd* (New York: Doubleday).

Riesman, D. (1958), 'Leisure and work in post-industrial society', in E. Larrabee and R. Meyersohn (eds), *Mass Leisure* (New York: The Free Press).

Riordan, J. (1982), 'Leisure: the state and the individual in the USSR', *Leisure Studies*, vol. 1 (January), pp. 65–80.

Roberts, K. (1974) 'The changing relationship between work and leisure', in I. Appleton (ed.), *Leisure Research and Policy* (Edinburgh: Scottish Academic Press).

Roberts, K. (1978), *Contemporary Society and the Growth of Leisure* (London: Longman).

Roberts, K. (1981), *Leisure*, 2nd edn (London: Longman).

Roberts, K., Clark, S. C., Cook, F. G., and Semeonoff, E. (1976), *On the Relationship between Work and Leisure: A Sceptical Note* (Liverpool: University of Liverpool, Department of Sociology).

Robins, K. and Webster, F. (1982), 'New technology: a survey of trade union response in Britain', *Industrial Relations Journal*, vol. 13 (Spring), pp. 7–26.

Ross, D. P. (1971), 'Leisure as a response to the technological change in the economic system', in S. M. A. Hameed and D. Cullen (eds), *Work and Leisure in Canada* (Edmonton: University of Alberta).

Roszak, T. (1979), *Person/Planet: The Creative Disintegration of Industrial Society* (London: Gollancz).

Rothman, S., and Mossman, G. (1972), *Computers and Society* (Chicago: Science Research Associates).

Rousseau, D. M. (1978), 'Relationship of work to nonwork', *Journal of Applied Psychology*, vol. 63, no. 4, pp. 513–17.

Sahlins, M. (1972), *Stone Age Economics* (Chicago: Aldine Atherton).

Salaman, G. (1971), 'Two occupational communities: examples of a remarkable convergence of work and non-work', *Sociological Review*, vol. 19 (August), pp. 389–407.

Salz, B. (1955), 'The human element in industrialization', *Economic Development and Cultural Change* (October), pp. 200–1.

Samson, E. (1972), *Future Perfect: Retirement Planning and Management* (London: Kimpton).

Samuel, N. (1967), 'Prediction and comparison in the sociology of leisure', paper presented to the British Sociological Association Conference, London.

Seeman, M. (1967), 'On the personal consequences of alienation in work', *American Sociological Review*, vol. 32 (April), pp. 273–85.

Seligman, B. B. (1965), 'On work, alienation and leisure', *American Journal of Economics and Sociology*, October, pp. 337–60.

Senker, P. (1981), 'Technical change, employment and international competition', *Futures*, vol. 13 (June), pp. 159–70.

Shamir, B. (1981), 'The workplace as a community: the case of British hotels', *Industrial Relations Journal*, vol. 12, no. 6, pp. 45–56.

Sheridan, J. (1982), 'Action sport: a Sports Council initiative for sports leadership', in A. J. Veal *et al.* (eds), *Work and Leisure* (London: Leisure Studies Association).

Sillitoe, K. K. (1969), *Planning for Leisure* (London: HMSO).

Simpson, R. L., and Simpson, I. H. (1960), 'Values, personal influence and occupational choice', *Social Forces*, December, pp. 116–35.

Smith, M. A., and Simpkins, A. F. (1980), *Unemployment and Leisure* (Salford: University of Salford, Centre for Leisure Studies).

Soule, G. (1956), *What Automation Does to Human Beings* (London: Sidgwick & Jackson).

Soule, G. (1957), 'The economics of leisure', *Annals of the American Academy of Political and Social Science*, September, pp. 16–24.

Spreitzer, E., and Snyder, E. (1974), 'Work orientation, meaning of leisure and mental health', *Journal of Leisure Research*, vol. 6, pp. 207–19.

Staines, G. L. (1980), 'Spillover versus compensation: a review of the literature on the relationship between work and nonwork', *Human Relations*, vol. 33, no. 2, pp. 111–30.

Stone, G. P. (1958), 'American sports: play and dis-play', in E. Larrabee and R. Meyersohn (eds), *Mass Leisure* (New York: The Free Press).

Stonier, T. (1980), 'Technological change and the future', in G. Cherry and A. S. Travis (eds), *Leisure in the 1980s: Alternative Futures* (London: Leisure Studies Association).

Strzeminska, H. (1966), 'Socio-professional structure and time-budgets', report to Sixth World Congress of Sociology, Evian.

Sutherland, W. C. (1957), 'A philosophy of leisure', *Annals of the American Academy of Political and Social Science*, September, pp. 1–3.

Szalai, A. (1972), *The Use of Time* (The Hague: Mouton).

Talbot, M. (1979), *Women and Leisure* (London: Sports Council).

Teague, R., and Erickson, C. (eds), (1974), *Computers and Society* (St Paul, Minn.: West).

Thornton, P., and Wheelock, V. (1979), 'What future for employment?', *Employee Relations*, vol. 1, no. 1.

Thornton, P., and Wheelock, V. (1980), 'Technology and employment: the prospects to 1990', *International Journal of Social Economics*, vol. 7, no. 1, pp. 24–36.

Tilgher, A. (1931), *Work: What it has Meant to Men through the Ages* (London: Harrap).

Toffler, A. (1980), *The Third Wave* (London: Collins).

Torbert, W., and Rogers, M. (1972), *Being for the Most Part Puppets: The Interaction of Men's Labor, Leisure and Politics* (Cambridge, Mass.: Schenkman).

Tucker, J. (1981), *Pipelayers: the Social World of a Community of Workmen*, Working Paper No. 16 (Durham: University of Durham, Department of Sociology).

Tunstall, J. (1962), *The Fishermen* (London: MacGibbon & Kee).

Veal, A. J. (1982), 'Work/leisure relationships: a closer look', paper presented to the Tenth World Congress of Sociology, Mexico City.

Veblen, T. (1925), *The Theory of the Leisure Class* (London: Allen & Unwin).

Vickerman, R. W. (1980), 'The new leisure society – an economic analysis', *Futures*, vol. 12, pp. 191–200.

Vincent, M., and Mayers, J. (1959), *New Foundations for Industrial Sociology* (Princeton, NJ: Van Nostrand).

Vogel, E. F. (1963), *Japan's New Middle Class* (Berkeley, Calif.: University of California Press).

Vogt, E. Z. (1955), *Modern Homesteaders* (Cambridge, Mass.: Harvard University Press).

Vontobel, K. (1945), *Das Arbeitsethos des deutschen Protestantismus* (Bern: Francke), quoted in N. Anderson (1961), *Work and Leisure* (London: Routledge & Kegan Paul).

Watts, A. C. (1981), 'Careers education and the informal economies', *British Journal of Guidance and Counselling*, vol. 9, no. 1.

Wax, R. H. (1958), 'Free time in other cultures', in W. Donahue *et al.* (eds), *Free Time: Challenge to Later Maturity* (Ann Arbor, Mich.: University of Michigan Press), pp. 3–16.

Weiss, P. (1960), 'A philosophical definition of leisure', in *Leisure in America: Blessing or Curse?*, American Academy of Political and Social Science Monograph No. 4 (New York: AAPSS).

Weiss, R. S., and Kahn, R. L. (1960), 'Definitions of work and occupations', *Social Problems*, Fall, pp. 142–50.

White, R. C. (1955), 'Social class differences in the use of leisure', *American Journal of Sociology*, September, pp. 145–50.

Wilensky, H. L. (1960), 'Work, careers and social integration', *International Social Science Journal*, no. 4, pp. 543–60.

Wilensky, H. L. (1964), 'Mass society and mass culture: interdependence or independence?', *American Sociological Review*, April, pp. 173–97.

Wilensky, H. L. (1981), *Family Life Cycle, Work, and the Quality of Life* (Berkeley, Calif.: University of California Institute of Industrial Relations).

Willener, A. (1967), 'French sociology and the problem of social engineering', paper presented to the British Sociological Association conference, London.

Willmott, P. (1971), 'Family, work and leisure conflicts among male employees', *Human Relations*, vol. 24 (December), pp. 575–84.

Wilson, J. (1980), 'Sociology of leisure', *Annual Review of Sociology*, vol. 6, pp. 21–40.

Young, M., and Willmott, P. (1973), *The Symmetrical Family* (London: Routledge & Kegan Paul).

Index